Young W
2004 POETRY CO

GW00493244

ONCE
A RHYME

IMAGINATION FOR
A NEW GENERATION

. . . Poetically Ever After
Vol IV
Edited by Steve Twelvetree

First published in Great Britain in 2004 by:
Young Writers
Remus House
Coltsfoot Drive
Peterborough
PE2 9JX
Telephone: 01733 890066
Website: www.youngwriters.co.uk

SB ISBN 1 84460 638 4

Foreword

Young Writers was established in 1991 and has been passionately devoted to the promotion of reading and writing in children and young adults ever since. The quest continues today. Young Writers remains as committed to engendering the fostering of burgeoning poetic and literary talent as ever.

This year's Young Writers competition has proven as vibrant and dynamic as ever and we are delighted to present a showcase of the best poetry from across the UK. Each poem has been carefully selected from a wealth of *Once Upon A Rhyme* entries before ultimately being published in this, our twelfth primary school poetry series.

Once again, we have been supremely impressed by the overall high quality of the entries we have received. The imagination, energy and creativity which has gone into each young writer's entry made choosing the best poems a challenging and often difficult but ultimately hugely rewarding task - the general high standard of the work submitted amply vindicating this opportunity to bring their poetry to a larger appreciative audience.

We sincerely hope you are pleased with our final selection and that you will enjoy *Once Upon A Rhyme . . . Poetically Ever After Vol IV* for many years to come.

Contents

Naomi Tawiah (9)   55
Sofia Nyman (9)   56
Louisa Tagziria (10)   56
Shannon Berry (9)   57
Sigrid Huld (9)   57

Fetlar Primary School, Shetland
James Boxall (8)   58
Rowan Boxall (10)   58
Tom Thomason (7)   59
Frank Coutts (9)   59

Gig Mill Primary School, Stourbridge
Daniel Sheppard (9)   60
Laura-Beth Green (9)   60
Sarah Bayliss (9)   61
Kathryn Hedar (9)   61
Jessica Watson (10)   62
Sophie Siviter (9)   62
Shelby Cartwright (10)   63
Alison Horton (9)   63
Jacob Gledhill (9)   64
Callum Scott (9)   64
Matthew Jones (9)   64
Jack Stanier (9)   65
Zoë Emery (9)   65
William Harding (9)   66
Matt Pugh (9)   66
Kieren Pratty (9)   67
Daniel Gilson (9)   67

Hampden Gurney Primary School, London
Tiyah Hernandez (8)   68
Renna Kassir (8)   68
Chioke Morgan Brown (9)   69
Paula Otalvora (9)   69
Abdullah Puri (8)   70
Noir El-Nour (8)   70
Richard Lewis (8)   70
Olivia Curtis (9)   71

Faisal Piracha (9)   71
Kieran George (9)   71
Baatar Sod-Uyanga (9)   72
Israa Fawaz (9)   72
Aaron Brown (9)   73
Shreeda Mehta (8)   73
Charlotte Kerr (9)   73
Zoe Pahne (8)   74
Jumana Ismail (7)   74
Joseph Howe (7)   74
Andrew Mitrousis (7)   75
Bonnie Heaton (7)   75
Gela Karumidze (7)   75
Megan Elie (8)   76
Taylor Green (8)   76
Stefan Svrdlin (8)   76
Ryan Welan (8)   77
Khamarl Christie (8)   77
Charlie Bishton-Worley (8)   77
Bahareh Nassiri (8)   78

Iwade Community Primary School, Kent
Georgia Harding (9)   78
Kieran Smith (8)   79
Ben Williams (7)   79
Simon Lawrence (9)   80
Jack Cooper (11)   80
Matthew Putnam (9)   81
Daniel Easton (8)   81
Adam Cox (8)   82
Zoe Whiffen (8)   82
Conner Millington (8)   83
Ellie Cooper (7)   83
Jasmin Kisnorbo (9)   83
Casey Stone (8)   84
Charlotte Mills (9)   84
David Easton (8)   85
Manny Latunde (9)   86
Emily Fitton (9)   87
Warren James (10)   87
Connor Edis (10)   88

Shaina Ormston (9)   89
Jack Anderson (10)   90
Daniel Elliott (9)   90
Jack Ince (10) & Jack Fitton (11)   91
Sophie Carmody (11)   91
Elizabeth Sheppard (11)   92
Charlotte Fisher (10)   92
Ryan Luker (10)   93
Jamie-Lee Smith (11)   93
Lauren Edwards (11)   93
Anna Marie Brookman (10)   94
Faye Easton (10)   94
Rachel Harrison (10)   95
James Hooper (11)   95
Eben Graham (10)   96
Sabrina Ormston (10)   96

Kincardine-in-Menteith Primary School, Blairdrummond
Courtney Ferguson (10)   97
James McBeath (11)   97
Madeleine Darby (10)   98
Fraser Graham (11)   98
Amanda Killen (9)   99
Jaime Buchanan (10)   99
Phil Aitken (8)   100
Teddi Anderson (10)   100
Andrew McLeod (11)   100
John Graham (7)   101
Louise Wilson (8)   101
Jack Brisbane (8)   102

Manor Primary School, Tamworth
Anisa Shareef (10)   102
Dale Jones (10)   103
Emily Church (11)   103
Jack Nelson (9)   104
Catherine White (11)   105
Jessica Tudor (9)   106
Megan Webb (9)   106
Connor Smith (9)   107
Sam Storey (11)   107

Lisa Poxon (11)	108
Amy Morris (11)	108
James Bennett (9)	109
Sarah Starkey (9)	109
Ganesh S Parmar (10)	110
Sophie Dixon (11)	110
Natalie Ayres (9)	111
Aiden Clarke (10)	111
Becky Milner (11)	112

Messingham Primary School, Scunthorpe

Courtney Frear (9)	113
Keiran Lindley (9)	113
Matthew Taylor (7)	113
Joshua Chamberlain	114
Oscar Smith (11)	114
Luke Fisher (9)	115
Jade Harniess (11)	115
Perdita-Jayne Lancaster (10)	116
Chris Welsh (10)	116
Georgia Clay (10)	117
Thomas Polkinghorne (10)	117
Shay Palmer (8)	118
Thomas Glencross (11)	118
Matthew Mettam (9)	118
Jake Crossland (9)	119
Andy Slater (8)	119
Jake Marshall (8)	119
Rebecca Catterick (8)	120
Rebecca Walters (8)	120
Rory Simpson (8)	120
Bethany Drewery (8)	120
Amy Cook (8)	121
Evie White (9)	121
Macaulay Farrell (8)	122
Emma Wrigley (8)	122
Max Alvy	123
Lauren Spreckley (8)	123
Maddison Withers (8)	123
Lauren Jarvill (8)	124
Eilish Brown (8)	124

Minard Primary School, Inveraray

North Mundham Primary School, Chichester

Jennifer McClelland (10)	148
Jordan Satturley (9)	148
Ellie Hutchings (11)	149
Alex Andrews (9)	149
Laura Kiely (11)	150
Emily Simpson (10)	150
Liberty Rosewarne (8)	151

St Albert's RC Primary School, Liverpool

Joshua Johnston (6)	151
Dylan Rose (7)	152
Faith Barton (9)	152
Kyra Edwards (6)	152
Aimee Lee (10)	153
Dimitri Manoussaridis (6)	153
Siobhan Mulligan (7)	154
Laura Morris (7)	154
Francesca Coggins (7)	154
Emilia Carden (7)	155
Sophie Richards (7)	155
Ashleigh Case (10)	155
Andrew Hardy (10)	156
Ciara Crosby (7)	156
Paul Carter (9)	157
Robyn Wall (7)	157
Brogan Davies (9)	158
Charlotte Bennett (7)	158
Jessica Hassell-Richardson (7)	159
Sean Mulligan (9)	159
Sheamus Brennan (7)	159
Leighton Williams (9)	160
Rebecca Furlong (7)	160
Joseph Williams (9)	161
Jamie Ennis (10)	161
Cheyenne Farrelly-Treanor (9)	162
Thomas Davies (10)	162
Jonathan Spittle (9)	163
Charlotte Jones (10)	163
Declan Barry (10)	164
Lucy McFarlane (10)	164
Ellie McCarthy (10)	165

St John's Primary School, Lincoln

St Teresa's Catholic Primary School, Wokingham

Hannah Jacklin (9)	180
Laura Thurston (10)	181
Laura Day (10)	181
Annie McKay (9)	181
Christopher Smith (9)	182
Thomas Eden (10)	183
Michael Ricketts (9)	183

The British International School of Stavanger, Norway

Benedicta Gibbs (8)	183
Katie Crosby (7)	184
Amy Gildert (8)	184
David Dixon (8)	185
Stuart Gray (7)	185
Michael Suguchev (9)	185
Joshua Brown (9)	186
Guendalina De Luigi (8)	187
Elise Damstra (9)	187
Clare Cuthbert (9)	187
Frances Jackson (8)	188
Christina Pedersen (8)	188
Becky Morrice (7)	189
Darren Maguire (7)	189
Sofie Reianes (7)	190
Calum Ferguson (7)	190
Ellen Thomas (8)	190
Jacob Fortes-Goldman (10)	191
Christopher Long (9)	191
Jade Joyce (8)	192
Christopher Nilsen (11)	192
Richard Phonbun (8)	192
Christina Nadeau (11)	193
Santhiya Manickavasakar (11)	193
Anna Surgucheva (11)	194
Katherine Wang (9	194
Andrew Hunter (10)	194
Emily Morrice (9)	195
Britt Lee Lövöy (10)	195
Callum Francis (10)	196
Magnus Hoie (11)	196
Nivetha Nantharuben (9)	197

Stefano Croatto (8)	197
Jack Sullivan (9)	197
Julia Sullivan (8)	198
Maiken Smylie (7)	198
Jon Toft (8)	199
Lise Laerdal Bryn (7)	199
Sønke Benz (8)	200

Willaston CE Primary School, Willaston

William Green (10)	200
William Mellor (10)	200
Hannah Bramley (9)	201
Philip Mellor (9)	201
Graham O'Sullivan (11)	202
Luke Homan (10)	203
Ben Cawley (9)	203
Rose Jones (11)	204
Joe Adamou (10)	204
Jennifer Ebbrell (11)	205
Calvin Deer (10)	205
Becky Smith (11)	206
Robert Eccles (11)	207
James Whitehouse (9)	207
Chris Hall (10)	208
Stephanie de Jonge (8)	208
Max Eastwood (11)	209
Tasha Whorton (10)	210
Emily Straiton (9)	210
Jonathan Crick (9)	211
George Wilkinson (9)	211
Robyn Whorton (8)	212
Tara Hatton (9)	212
Bethan Currie (8)	213

The Poems

Friends

Friends are kind and good to me, they are hard to find.
Friends will help me whatever may be
Friends look after me, everyone can see
We can look after each other, even my brother
Friends play with me, what fun that may be.

Klara Kiernan (10)

If I Could Hear . . .

If I could hear
A petal growing
If I could hear
A person thinking

If I could hear
A ladybird singing
If I could hear
A book opening

If I could hear
A cat walking
If I could hear
A leaf dropping

If I could hear
A tongue wagging
If I could hear
A tree whistle

If I could hear
A wasp humming
If I could hear
A fish swimming.

Ify Iwobi (10)

A Storm In An Irish Field

The atrocious sky heaved a silky black sheet of darkness,
Like an owl swooping for the kill,
Over the lonely field.

The wind whooshed with rage and the thunder boomed with terror,
Lightning bolts sabotaged trees and set on fire,
Fires of fear and death!

The pitter-patter of rain became splish, splash
As it became heavier and heavier
It became ice spikes and hail . . .
Boom! Boom!
Lightning ignites!

Luca Dyke (9)

The Biker

He went to school on a bike, he did
On a bike he went to school.
In spite of all his friends would say,
On a summer's morn, on a boiling day
On a bike he went to school!
And when the bike turned in the dirt
Everyone shouted, 'You'll get hurt!'
He whispered, 'My bike is tiny,
My bike is big! I don't care at all!
On a bike I'll go to school!'
Here and there, here and there
Was the place where the biker lived,
His head was red and his legs were blue
And he went to school on a bike.

Suean Busby (11)

Hunger

It's more terrible than feared armies
It's listened to more than anybody
Yet gives no commands
First feeling at birth
And the last at death.
Hunger.

Is it what only poor people feel?
Or is it able to catch everyone?
Does it have a creed or colour, age or size?

It's when my mouth waters, stomach grumbles,
Like a restless lion.
Books call it a strong desire for food.
Presidents call it a difficult problem.
It has a mind of its own.

I can't think while I'm hungry.
I'm lost.
Everything I touch I compare with food.
Really hungry people can't think either.
Imagine if the world was hungry,
Food would be its only thought.
What if Shakespeare had been hungry -
What would we have lost?

Devastating stories are often heard
Of starving children dying.
Only one person to save us all now -
Our almighty God.

Kanyiha Mbogori (14)

My Family

Meet my family.
My mum doesn't like the feel of bubblegum,
But she likes the taste of it, yum-yum.
My dad shouts very loud when he's mad,
That's when we get sad.
My little brother's naughty towards my mother,
My mum gets a rest at the weekends because he sleeps
                                    at his grandmother's.
Me, I love to splash around in the sea,
I also like to ski.
My big brother loves to help my mother,
Because she's so great, she's like no other.
My big sis said to Miss,
'Give me a kiss.'
My dog went for a jog,
In the misty fog.
My hamster is a gangster,
With a lot of fur.
This is my family who I will love
Forever and ever.

Carly Mason (11)

Henry's Pets

In his bedroom Henry kept . . .
Ten fish swimming in a tank
Nine hamsters running on a wheel
Eight cats sleeping on the rug
Seven pythons slithering on the floor
Six ants that dig on the farm
Five dogs chasing the cats
Four pigs lazy and fat
Three white mice
Two donkeys who live in the world
And one guess what?

Henry McDonald

My Cat

My cat
is agile
and healthy
after a meal.

My cat
is soft
and cute
after a sleep.

My cat
is quiet
and calm
after a walk.

My cat
is the best
in the world.

Georgina Ely (9)

My Adventures

I've been eaten by many things,
Fish with jaws and birds with wings,
I've jumped on vines and crawled on floors,
Crept upstairs and gone through doors.

I shoot monsters and I get keys,
I save the nice and shoot the fleas,
But when will I get my fame
On my video game?

Violet Macdonald (10)

Windy Rain

Wind is grey,
It looks like clouds in the sky,
It sounds like a wolf howling,
It tastes like tree bark,
It feels like an iceberg in the sea,
The wind is horror.

Rain is indigo,
It looks like a rainbow,
It sounds like laughter,
It tastes like the universe,
It feels like dandelions,
Rain is *joy*.

Chuka Iwobi (8)

Favourite Sport

Basketball is my favourite sport,
I like the way we dribble up and down the court.
I like the way we bounce the ball upon and down,
I like the way we turn around and touch the ground.
I chucked my hands up in the air,
The crowd was gasping everywhere.
I slam-dunked the ball into the hoop,
At the same time it did a loop-the-loop.
When I score,
My friends cheer more and more.

Harry Lewis-Jones (9)

The Sun

A ball of blasting fire
A ball of blasting flame
This ball is one with which you could not play a game.

It floats above the Earth
Giving us our light
Some people try to reach it using all their might.

No person who lives now has been to this place
It would be great and fun,
But no one can go to the wonderful *sun*.

Sophie Morgan (10)

Balloons

My mum bought me a shiny, red balloon,
I kept it safe in Dad's stockroom.
When I played with it outside,
It started to tumble,
My sister was jealous,
She made it rumble.
I let it go high in the air,
It went so far out there!
I ran so very, very fast,
It bobbed and it squiggled
But I caught it at last!
I threw it up high
Right into the sun -
I never knew balloons
Could be such fun.
I threw it far away,
I knew it had gone.
Would it return one day?

Kudzai Tunduwani (9)

A Vampire

A vampire in the night
With a vicious bite, bite, bite
Ooh, what a fright
A vampire in the night
With sharp teeth of white, white, white
Ooh, what a fright
A vampire in the night.

A vampire in the night
Better not get in a fight, fight, fight
Ooh, what a fright, a vampire in the night
Spreading his cape like a kite, kite, kite
Ooh, what a fright
A vampire in the night.

He soars into the sky at midnight, midnight
Ooh, what a fright
A vampire in the night
A vampire
A vampire
A vampire in the night.

Sarah Larkin & Rachel Oliphant (11)

My Dog

My dog
Sleeps like a log
My dog is noisy
He is old and fat
My dog is thirteen
He is white
My dog is called Alfie
And I love him.

Linsey Walsh (7)

The Classroom

The classroom is a roaring place
children are always shouting
there's no peace

I hear children bellow
like there's no tomorrow
pens digging through the paper
there's no peace

Children are quieter
in the playground
sometimes, I think

Please teachers
stop them
I want peace.

Josh Bannister (12)

Spring

Springtime is a time for happiness
for laughter and for joy.
Birds tweeting, people singing,
praising for the coming of spring.
Flowers sprouting, bursting blossom,
the smell of daises growing.
Grass swaying in the air,
the sun layers the sky everywhere.
Smells drifting by to brighten up the day.
Colours electrify the sky.
All because of spring.

Kathryn Baum (10)

Apple Pie

The teacher made an apple pie
on the feast of May.
The teacher made an apple pie
on a Thursday.
The teacher made an apple pie,
she filled it with chilli sauce,
and egg and a snack
and lots of force.
She squashed it, she kicked it,
She liked it, she mixed it.

Nicky Monroe-Meares (7)

If Only . . .

If only clouds were candyfloss
And they always rained sherbet lemons
If only my house was made of sweets
And snakes carried choccy instead of venom

If only water was lemonade
And pencils were seaside rock
If only teachers were novelty chocolates
And watches were candy clocks

If only books were made of wafer
And the sun was pineapple ice cream
'Hey, where am I?' I get up and say
It must have been a dream!

Stephanie Edwards (10)
Abbey Junior School, Darlington

My Teacher!

My teacher is very glad,
She usually is very mad,
She dances in the middle of the room,
See, like she's over the moon,

Really hope she'll look at me,
She's really funny,
She gives us money,
She's really cool,
She used a tool
To fix my friend's teddy,
That's my teacher,
She's a very weird creature!

Emma Weedy (10)
Abbey Junior School, Darlington

My Teddy

When I go to bed
I have to have my teddy
He's brown and white
He holds a kite
And his name is Freddy.

He makes me go to sleep you see
He's nice and soft and cuddles me
He's fluffy, soft and made of wool
But my other teddies are kind of dull.

Freddy is my best teddy
I love him very much
I wish I never said that now
Because I love another teddy called Butch.

Josie Allenby (10)
Abbey Junior School, Darlington

There Is A Monster Under My Bed

There is a monster under my bed,
Going to sleep is what I dread.
Then at night when I am sleeping,
He comes out just peep, peep, peeping.
He creeps downstairs and raids the fridge,
Goes into the garden and crosses the bridge.
He has a quick dip in the pond,
But comes indoors before very long.
In the morning when I wake, Mum shouts,
'Where's all the food for goodness sake!'
Yelling and shouting comes from downstairs.
'Gone . . . all the apples, grapes and pears!'
But then when I look right under my bed,
'There's . . . nothing there anymore!'
'Ah, but look behind you!' a chill voice said.
And there's monster prints all over the floor.

Harriet Endersby (11)
Abbey Junior School, Darlington

Teachers

Miss Cunningham our new teacher of 6F,
She's a wicked teacher at school,
Mrs Oliver who's in teacher training
Is really stylish and cool!

Mrs Shaw, Mrs Johnson and Mrs Tweddle,
All educate Year 6 too,
They make learning fun; it's all just begun,
For everyone, including you!

Mr Ford's the best head teacher,
The best in creation,
He is hardly every strict,
I'd say he's the most chilled out in the nation!

Naomi Mackenzie (11)
Abbey Junior School, Darlington

Nails

My nails are stubby and small,
All round like a little paper ball.

My mum's are so long,
They prick me like a prong.

My dad's are square,
Not like a bear's
Because bear's are pointy and strong.

My brother's are little,
But very brittle.

My friend's are sticky,
All so gritty

And there are all the nails I know!

Kate Pilbeam (11)
Abbey Junior School, Darlington

My School Teachers

My maths teacher is called Mrs Snore,
She really is a bore,
She makes me fall asleep
And end up in a heap,
Lying on the floor.

My PE teacher is called Mr Fit,
He makes me forget my kit,
He really is nice,
But eats his pet mice,
That fabulous Mr Fit.

Emma Wright & Jo Lamb (11)
Abbey Junior School, Darlington

Seal Haiku

Seals that swim the sea
Riding, gliding through the deep
Searching for their souls.

Liam Durham (11)
Abbey Junior School, Darlington

Moon, Moon

Moon, moon, how bright can you be?
Every night I wait to see
Your gorgeous rays
Magnificent light
I wonder how you could be so bright
Your whispy white surface
So clean, so pure
Shimmering your light upon the Earth.

Moon, moon, how do you get your light?
It's so stunning it hurts my sight
You give me such a shocking surprise
How do you change your shape and size?
It's fabulous
It's marvellous
I wonder how you change?

Moon, moon, why do you hide your side?
You've got to show your face with honour and pride
Playing hide-and-seek behind a cloud
You must think yourself very proud
Travelling the sky without a sound
Moon, moon, you are full of life's mysteries to be found.

Kelly Stracey (10)
Abel Smith Primary School, Greencoats

The Moon

The moon is the jewel of the skies,
In which its light never dies,
Lord of the night,
Shining bright,
The moon is the jewel of the skies.

The moon appears just as it pleases
And disappears on runaway breezes,
In its silver boat,
Always afloat,
The moon appears just as it pleases.

The moon is the king amongst stars,
Ruling afar,
It appears in the night,
Bursting with light,
The moon is the king amongst stars.

Ryan Dunn (10)
Abel Smith Primary School, Greencoats

The Moonlight

M other said the moon was made of cheese
O ther people disagree
O h, the moon is lovely
N ow I know it's not made of cheese
L ight from the moon shows animals their way
I like the moon in every way
G o outside at the dead of night and see for yourself
H appy people love the moon
T ime to say goodbye to the moon, for the sun is rising.

Holly Shilston (10)
Abel Smith Primary School, Greencoats

I Wonder What The Moon Is?

At night, I look out of my bedroom window,
I look up at the moon,
I wonder,
What is the moon?

Is it a massive ball of silver glowing fire?
Is it a floating ball of lumpy cottage cheese?
Or maybe it is an alien spaceship stuck in outer space?
Is it a huge, round mirror, reflecting the sun's glorious rays?
Is it a hunched, old man trudging across the sky?

I look out of my window again
And I think, Is it a guardian angel
Sent to watch over us whilst we sleep?

Sam Ring (10)
Abel Smith Primary School, Greencoats

The Moon

The moon is like a big, round ball
And it shines from big to very small,
A lot or not at all.
The moon is like a shiny star
That always follows you wherever you are.
The moonlight glows like a disco ball
In a hall.

The moon is like a grey-haired nan,
That likes sending you to sleep
And when she's read a bedtime story
You won't make a peep.
When I think of the moonlight,
I think of a torch leading the way.
The moon will always be there, somewhere.

Cherie Matthews (10)
Abel Smith Primary School, Greencoats

The Moon

The moon is a glittering ball,
Shining down on every wall,
The moon is a silver spy,
Watching people as they lie,
The moon is a special speck,
As it glows on the world's neck,
The moon is a jewel in the skies,
It's a valuable light that never dies,
The moon is a ballet dancer,
Gracefully flying, like a real prancer,
The moon is a magical friend,
Her friendship that will never end,
The moon is a beautiful spotlight,
Shining out, ever so bright,
The moon is all of these things,
If you look closer.

Carla Cleaver (10)
Abel Smith Primary School, Greencoats

Moonlight

M agnificent
O ld
O utstanding
N oble
L ovely
I mpeccable
G lorious
H appy
T his is the moon that shines upon me.

Joanna Freeman (10)
Abel Smith Primary School, Greencoats

Moon Poem

The moon makes me think,
of a light bulb hanging on the ceiling of the sky.
The moon, up there so high.

The moon makes me feel,
warm inside,
sitting there alone outside.

The moon makes me think,
of a glow worm,
that does not wriggle or squirm.

The moon makes me feel,
not alone,
it follows me everywhere
so I'm not on my own.

Emma Pearce (10)
Abel Smith Primary School, Greencoats

What I Think Of The Moon

Our moon is a glistening ball
Of tasty Swiss cheese.
It plays hide-and-seek
Like six-year-old children.
It follows the sun like a spy
Hiding behind the Earth.
A glowing light bulb in a black room
When it's a bulbous shape
It looks like a man's face.
That's what I think of the moon.

Laurence Kingdon (10)
Abel Smith Primary School, Greencoats

I Think Of The Moon

I think of the moon,
When it's dark at night,
Watching over me,
Going over me, giving everything light.

I think of the moon,
When I'm cold, on my own,
It warms me up,
From head to toe.

I think of the moon,
In my dreams,
Glittering and glistening,
It always gleams.

I think of the moon,
Every single night,
Until the sun comes up
And shines its gleaming bright light.

Emma Davies (10)
Abel Smith Primary School, Greencoats

My Moon

The moon is a giant pearl
that has fallen from its clam.
It is the world's night light,
ever shining.
The moon is a boat sailing on an open sea
sailing round and round looking after me.
It keeps me safe in the dark, dark night
giving me a bit more light.
The moon is always coming and going
like it is playing tag.
But at the end of the day
he always comes back to see me.

Sophie Campbell Blake (10)
Abel Smith Primary School, Greencoats

What Is The Moon?

Mum, what is the moon?
Is it a diamond in the sky,
or is it a runaway train passing by?

Dad, what is the moon?
Is it a light bulb that turns on and off,
or is it a disco ball that the star dance to non-stop?

Grandad, what is the moon?
Is it a ghostly galleon that sails across the dark seas,
or is it a magic crystal ball that moves along the breeze?

The moon could be all these things,
but the best thing it can do,
is be our moon.

Charlotte I'Anson (10)
Abel Smith Primary School, Greencoats

The Moon

The moon is as pale as a ghost
but what I really like the most
is the way it shimmers and brightens up the night
as it glistens with all its might.

The moon makes me feel so alive
that when I step outside I break into the hand jive
it gives me a warm feeling inside
as it travels on its journey far and wide.

The moon always leads the way
even when you're in a car on a dark day
the moon follows you everywhere
but in the day it's very rare.

The moon is just so precious to us
so when it hurts your eyes, don't make a fuss
when you can see the moon is here
you won't have to worry, or have a fear.

Eleanor Froud (10)
Abel Smith Primary School, Greencoats

My Darling Sugar

Very sweet,
Your lovely taste,
That is so sweet,
I love you so,
Your sugary taste,
That is why I know,
My own darling sugar.

Sugar, sugar,
Quiet, so sweet,
Your sugary dots
That are so small,
I drink it with anything,
Anything at all,
My own sugar
Is not ordinary,
But a darling sugar is
Always a darling sugar.

Tosin Baiyeroju (10)
All Saints' Church School, Nigeria

My Headmistress

A great woman indeed
Mother of children
The headmistress of headmistresses
The mistress of teaching
Not the mistress of teachers
We salute our headmistress
Our jarred name she eradicated
And fame she brought in return -
Through her hand work which
Will never be forgotten
The progress she restored
We salute you my dear headmistress
A strong woman indeed.

Olaoluwa Denloye (9)
All Saints' Church School, Nigeria

My Dad's Old Beetle Car

Oh, my dad's old Beetle car
You are so old
You have been working for so long
That you now malfunction
Instead of sounding like a good car
You sound like a grinding machine
Instead of moving like a good car
You move like a crippled one-legged man
Oh, my dad's old Beetle car
I used to like you before
But now the way you work puts me off
Oh, my dad's old Beetle car.

Adesuyi Oluwamolawa (9)
All Saints' Church School, Nigeria

My Friend

My friend
My own dear friend
Loving and kind
Honest and dear
My own dear friend
Helpful at all times
Truthful in all things
My own dear friend
A friend indeed
A friend in need
My own dear friend
Oh! My friend
Closer than a brother.

Sharon Alfred (10)
All Saints' Church School, Nigeria

Oh My Dear Father

Oh my dear father
One in a million you are,
A man so caring, like a woman,
You are more precious to me than anymore.

Oh my dear father,
So compassionate and loving,
So gentle and a good listener,
How can I forget you - Father?

Oh my dear father,
How wonderful you are,
Backing me when I was young,
Your gentle touch is more than that of a mother.

Oh my dear father
Excited when I make progress.
Always correct in love, my mistakes,
How can I forget you my dear father?

Ajele Eniola (9)
All Saints' Church School, Nigeria

Family And Friends

Family and friends
I love my family
I love my daddy and my mummy
I love my three sisters
We are a wonderful family
I have good friends
I love playing with them
Blue, red and pink
Are my best friends' colours
Oh, how I wish we could have more fun together
With my family and friends.

Oluwayomi Oduwole (8)
All Saints' Church School, Nigeria

Time

Time is a precious jewel,
It ticks and tocks,
Walking twelve kilometres in twenty-four hours,
Time waits for no man.

The way you spend your time,
Is the way you spend your life.
Time wasted can't be regained,
Time regained can't be wasted.

If you are wise, then spend it wisely,
If you are foolish, spend it lavishly,
If you are lazy, spend it sleeping,
Remember, the way you spend your time determines who you are.

Oluwabukunmi Aina (10)
All Saints' Church School, Nigeria

The Park

I often wish, when lying in the dark
Snug as a bug
In my bed, in my house
I was still playing in the park

Lying upon the grass
Beneath the sky
Watching clouds go by
Like fences on glass

I do not ever need to sing
Myself to sleep
Or try hard at counting sheep

Instead I fly the night air
On a swing
A comet flashing through the dark
I often wish to sleep in the park.

Jade Williams (11)
All Saints' C in W Primary School, Wrexham

When I Saw A Shooting Star

When I saw a shooting star,
I wished to play for Newcastle,
To score the winning goal against United.

I can just see myself dribbling past players,
I can hear the commentators,
'He has got past the midfield,
Past the defence!
Then it's one on one with the keeper!

He shoots! He scores!'
The crowd go wild,
I heard them shout, 'David! David!'
All the players came and congratulated me.

I think to myself,
It will never happen.
That was my dream,
That was when I saw a shooting star.

David Nelson (10)
All Saints' C in W Primary School, Wrexham

The Long Journey

I'm leaving my family, where will I go?
Images of my journey passing by.
Trickling streams, gleaming in the morning light,
And huge old trees swaying in the breeze gently,
The smell of freshly-cut grass licking the air,
What a sight!

I'm leaving my family, where will I go?
Images of my journey passing by.
A train taking the children to a safer place,
Away from the fighting and war,
Children crying because their parents have been
Left behind, to a death sentence.
What a horrible sight!

Amy Britner (11)
All Saints' C in W Primary School, Wrexham

The Journey Of The Evacuee

The platform, dark and foreboding, awaits the first arrival
of the day.
A mother, stooped with grief, tears trickling from her eyes like the
drizzle of a lonely cloud, waits for the child-taking train.
The daughter, unknowing and unaware, follows behind her grief-
stricken mother who carries a burden of sadness; a sack of rocks
pushing her shoulders down.
The heavy engine heaves its way into the station, almost as though it
knows the sad but life-saving task ahead of it. The mother holds her
child tight, smelling her hair one last time, trying to frame the picture of
her daughter in her mind.
The daughter cautiously steps onto the train, waving her mother
goodbye, attempting bravely to hold back the volcano of emotion
threatening to erupt.
The young girl hangs dumbly out of the window, not realising the true
meaning of this long journey.
As the train pulls away, a squadron of unfamiliar planes passes
overhead, swooping and diving, swallows in the sun.
A little time later, a factory looms out of the fog, sprawling like a
powerful army, looking down on the surrounding countryside.
Smoke explodes from its tall chimneys in strange mushroom shapes,
disappearing as quickly as it appeared.
A tree on the bank of the railway, silent and watchful, waves in the
wind; a crowd of cheering supporters.
A medieval tower, tall and terrifying once, now crumbled and ruined,
lies on the mountainside, a stone from the sky.
A tunnel, like the open mouth of a dragon, beckoning to the train like a
spider to a fly.
The train slows, entering the dark throat of the dragon, pushing the
darkness aside, knowing its precious cargo's need for safety.
As the train emerges into the light, the girl breathes a sigh of relief.
Soon, the guard appears, a father reassuring a child that the journey is
nearly over.

Christopher Hitchcock (11)
All Saints' C in W Primary School, Wrexham

A Fight For Freedom

Where was the horse and the rider?
Where was the horn that was blown?
They passed like rain on a mountain,
Like wind in a meadow.
The days have gone down in the west,
Behind the hills, into shadow.

For ourselves there is no hope,
This is the final act of our time,
To give time to destroy the evil that marshals before us.
For there may come a day when the strength of men fails . . .
An hour of wolves before the age of men comes crashing down . . .
But it will not be this day! . . . This day we fight . . .
For freedom, for valour and for the free peoples of our land.

So a last alliance of men charged against the armies of evil . . .
There to do battle with death.
Swarms of arrows form swallows that pierce the sky like daggers . . .
They then swarm down tearing into unsuspecting victims below.
Yelps of pain . . . blood-curdling screams.
As hour after hour, our enemies hail rains of arrows.

Clattering of sword of good against shield of evil.
Shrill screams of swords carve into their victims.
But in truth, this is just a diversion to give time.
After all, what can men do against such evil?
Against foes that wield the machine of war with pride,
Against foes that burn up our world in the fires of industry . . .
That oppose us with the sword, the spear and the iron fist.

This is just a battle to give time.
Time enough to destroy the evil that marshals before us.

Joseph Ford-Brown (11)
All Saints' C in W Primary School, Wrexham

Melting Away!

I wrote my name in the condensation,
    on the window, then rubbed it out.
I looked outside, the snow hadn't been touched,
    except from a little bird's footprints.
I grabbed my coat and put on my wellies,
    I was still in my pyjamas but I didn't care.
The snow beneath my feet crunched and cracked,
    it felt great to be out, even though it was cold.
I had fun in the snow making snow angels, snowmen
    and having snowball fights.
I went to bed that night very tired
    and couldn't wait to have fun tomorrow.
I woke up like the morning before,
    I ran to the window, but the only bit of snow
    left was on top of the snowman's hat!
Mum said that the snow had melted,
    that it had gone!

Emily Morgan (11)
All Saints' C in W Primary School, Wrexham

Wonderland

Roses are red, violets are blue,
You are sweet and I am too.
You love me and I love you,
I am beauty and so are you.
I am in wonderland and so are you.
This is a place where you and me have a great time.
You're the best and so am I.
Welcome to wonderland!

Victoria Jurgens (8)
Antwerp International School, Belgium

My Dog

When I go home
I see my dog.
He is so delighted to see me
He is my dog.
He is so big, white and furry
He is my dog.
He plays football, he fetches
He is my dog.
When he goes for a walk
He pulls on the lead like a wild animal
He is my dog.
He sneaks into the house like a mouse
He is my dog.
He runs away for miles and miles
Maybe one day he will go to England
But now it's too late because he is dead
That was my dog.

Zane Mehta (10)
Antwerp International School, Belgium

Fairies

The light closes in everyone's house,
The watch strikes 12am,
The fairies come out,
Dancing like ballerinas,
Tiptoeing across the floor,
With their wings flapping around
And their hair gliding on the floor,
They fly around children,
They fly around toys,
Spreading around their magic,
Around and around,
When the sun rises they all hide
And start again,
When the sun set down.

Arya Mehta (10)
Antwerp International School, Belgium

The Thing Under My Bed

There is a thing under my bed
That makes noises all night long,
I wonder what it could be?
A monster, a ghost or a scary cat
Or maybe even my neighbour's dog?
There is a smell coming from under my bed,
It is a horrible, awful smell,
I could not describe how it smells,
I am scared!
I am shivering under my covers,
I shout for my dad!
He dashes up the stairs,
He opens the door and turns on the light,
He sees me standing on the ceiling,
He saw a monster wearing a big sweater and growling,
The light scared the monster,
The monster ran away,
That was the last I ever saw of the monster.

Luke Levan (11)
Antwerp International School, Belgium

Friendship

The only ship that can't sink
Is friendship.
Friends are always there
To laugh at your jokes
And help you sail through life.
If the ship sunk
There would be a battle,
There would be canons flying in the sky.
The ship would break in two,
Then finally the ship would go back together
And if it didn't mend, the ship would never really sink
Because if you ever get a friend
They will always stay in your heart.

Sarah Pinkham (10)
Antwerp International School, Belgium

Hamsters

I smell food,
I smell food
It's a carrot
And sunflower seeds,
It's mine,
Only mine,
I run as fast as a train.
It looks like I'm never going to reach
To the food plate.
I'm touching the floor
With my paws,
The floor is cold.
I close my eyes
And I count to five,
One,
Two,
Three,
Four,
Five.
When I open my eyes,
I realise I am in Iceland!
Argh! I screamed,
I counted to five again,
Again, one,
Two,
Three,
Four,
Five.
Finally
I was touching the food,
But when I ate a sunflower seed
I noticed it was a dream.

Jessica Chadwick (10)
Antwerp International School, Belgium

My Dog

I hear him howling
He's coming, he's bounding
I hear him breathing
That's what I hear
I know he's coming
I know he's near
My dog's so cute
My dog's so smooth
My dog's so wild
He's in the groove
He eats his food
When he's in the mood
But all I know is that
He is so good
I love my dog
So very much
He's something
I can always touch.

Nathalie Hussa (10)
Antwerp International School, Belgium

Witches

Wand
Mag*i*c
Talented
Cauldrons
Hats
Mast*E*r of spells
Tran*S*formations.

Kristen Morse (8)
Antwerp International School, Belgium

Look Beyond The Outside

I wish you would look beyond
The outside, you might be fat
I might be thin,
You might run fast,
I might run slowly,
But what matters most is to look beyond

The outside,
Look at the inside,
Look at the heart and soul,
Don't put people in the blues,
Make people cheerful not in despair,
So remember what matters most
Is to look beyond the outside,
Beyond the outside.

Rohaan Rayani (10)
Antwerp International School, Belgium

Summer Beauty

Summer, summer, my favourite season,
The sun is shining, the ocean is breathing.
Swimming with friends, at last my dream's come true
And once again I'm smiling happily.

Sprinting along the rough, scorching sand,
I still smile as the dolphins dance a mile.
Building sandcastles makes my eyes shine bright,
Near the rocks, tropical fish swim in schools,
As crabs snap away in the light blue sea.

Summer, summer, my favourite season,
The sun is shining, the ocean is breathing.

Neveen Ahmad (8)
Antwerp International School, Belgium

Manchester United

'Glory, glory Man United,'
The smell of hot dogs waft,
Packets of crisps crinkle,
Furious feet stamp,
Sweat,
D
R
I
P
S,
Tongues taste excited, suspense,
A slidy, plasticy, greasy seat,
Green grass glinting,
Red dots scurrying after the golf ball,
Hole in one,
Man U score,
Yeah!

Lloyd Grieve (11)
Antwerp International School, Belgium

Sounds

The tiniest sound in the world must be
an ant crawling on the ground

The noisiest sound in the world must be
soldiers marching to battle

The spookiest sound in the world must be
a ghost stealing stuff from me

The happiest sound in the world must be
my brother laughing with me.

Umang Parikh (6)
Antwerp International School, Belgium

Friendship

Friend, friend, friendship
Is like a beautiful flower
That will grow fast and happy if you give it a chance,
Friend, friend, friendship
Is what you need.

Sophie Hulling (9)
Antwerp International School, Belgium

Snake

S mall
N oble
A wesome
K illing its prey
E normous.

Matthew Mikrut (9)
Antwerp International School, Belgium

My Mother

Her hair, black as midnight,
Her cheeks like tiny roses,
Her lips as soft as cotton,
Her skin as smooth as silk,
'Who?' you may ask, 'Who is this person?'
'She,' I say, 'she is my mother.'

Sana Kothari (9)
Antwerp International School, Belgium

Lion

Lives in the grassy plains
Runs fast
Big animal
Strong animal
Likes to hunt
Lazy
Little fur
Sharp claws
Roars
Carnivorous
'King of the jungle'
Rare
Feared
Majestic and
Proud.

Shawn Mehta (8)
Antwerp International School, Belgium

Music To My Ears

Waves come crashing
To the shore,
Horses trotting across
Fields afar,
Chirping birds at
The crack of dawn
Is music to my ears.
Shall I go on?

Baby's laughter,
Father's snores,
Playing children's lively calls
Is music to my ears.
I'll carry on!

Rishaad Rayani (9)
Antwerp International School, Belgium

Sports!

Sports! Sports! I love sports!
Sports are fun.

Fun sports are football, baseball, basketball and soccer,
I love being outside, catching the football, hitting the baseball,
Shooting the basketball and kicking the soccer ball.

It is all very exciting.

Being with my friends is also fun. We like to kick the soccer ball,
Throw and catch the football, shoot the basketball
And pitch, hit and field the baseball.

My dad is good at sports. He loves throwing the football,
Pitching the baseball, shooting the basketball
And saving the soccer ball . . . all with me!

Sports! Sports! I love sports!

Ben Carroll (9)
Antwerp International School, Belgium

Sounds

The tiniest sound in the world must be
a mouse squeaking really quietly

The noisiest sound in the world must be
a basketball game that I'm going to see with my family

The spookiest sound in the world must be
a ghost flying in the night-time sky scaring me and my family

The happiest sound in the world must be
me and my little sister laughing together.

Abby Laszewski (6)
Antwerp International School, Belgium

Sounds

The tiniest sound in the world must be
a cat sleeping on a car beside me

The noisiest sound in the world must be
when my sisters are screaming outside at me

The spookiest sound in the world must be
a vampire biting a tree

The happiest sound in the world must be
my cat and me chatting about me.

Simon Van Ooteghem (6)
Antwerp International School, Belgium

Sounds

The tiniest sound in the world must be
a mouse squeaking in the forest

The noisiest sound in the world must be
a lion roaring in the zoo

The spookiest sound in the world must be
a ghost singing songs while sitting on the trees

The happiest sound in the world must be
birds singing on the house

The funniest sound in the world must be
a frog saying, *'Goo goo'* at me.

Daichi Maeyama (6)
Antwerp International School, Belgium

Sounds

The tiniest sound in the world must be
a mouse squeaking.

The noisiest sound in the world must be
an aeroplane taking off for me.

The spookiest sound in the world must be
a ghost scaring me.

The happiest sound in the world must be
my music playing loudly out the window at me.

Leticia Luokkanen (6)
Antwerp International School, Belgium

The Lazy Polar Bear!

There was once a very lazy polar bear
Who just about sleeping did care

So he snored and snored,
Slept and slept,

Until a fantasy dream he had
That he was king and made all humans glad.

He removed his laziness like a weed
And worked hard for his dream to succeed.

So he left his lazy days
Which made the world around him gaze.

Rishabh Kothari (10)
Antwerp International School, Belgium

Cats And Dogs

Cats are cute and calm,
While dogs are messy and playful.
Cats have nice long claws to scratch you,
But dogs have big paws to push you down.
Cats love to chew on mice,
I think that dogs are pretty nice to mice.
Dogs love to go on walks,
But cats just like to wander off by themselves.
The only thing they have in common
Is that they *love* to be with their owner,
You!

Karen Luokkanen (10)
Antwerp International School, Belgium

My Alsatian!

I had an Alsatian that went on vacation
Well at least that's what I heard
But I thought my Alsatian was on probation
And that just seemed absurd
So I went out there looking
And saw him there woofing
And went and gave him a hug
I brought him back home
And gave him a bone
And he fell asleep on the rug.

Juliette Hoffmann (9)
Antwerp International School, Belgium

The Snowman

I made a snowman,
Just like a human.
Taller than my sister.
Born in winter.
Kinder than a cat,
He has a lovely hat.
He is very pretty,
Let's have milk tea,
He is really funny,
He is really chubby,
He's good at art,
Because he's smart.
I am his very good friend
And I think it'll never, ever end!
We can meet every year!
I am waiting over here!

Keiko Kubonoya (9)
Antwerp International School, Belgium

In Praise Of Summer

I love summer's wonderful weather,
Summer, summer, you're so cool,
Summer, summer, we play outside,
Summer, summer, the sun never dies.

I love summer for a cold drink,
Summer is the best season of all.

Summer's ice cream and surfing,
Summer is the best and you can't get a rest,
With all the activities to do,
You have to stop for a drink.

Liam Carfrae (8)
Burham CE Primary School, Rochester

In Praise Of Summer

Summer, summer, you are the best,
Summer, summer, you never rest,
Summer, summer, you shine on me,
Summer, summer, you make me happy.

Summer, summer, you make me feel great,
Summer, summer, you have a bright face in the sky,
Summer, summer, you shine on my face,
Summer, summer, you are so great,
Summer, summer, you make the world a better place.

The weather is very sunny,
Here and there,
You don't get much rain,
But you'd better beware of the rain in the air.

Aimee Roddam (8)
Burham CE Primary School, Rochester

In Praise Of Summer

Summer, summer, I can't get enough
Summer, summer, we love you a lot
Summer, summer, in the hot air
I got up so early I'm going to declare
I opened the door and twirled and swirled
And smelt the lovely summer air.

When summer is here, when summer is here
Bees buzz past.
On the beach the tide comes in
It makes my friends happy to watch the sea
And enjoy their ice creams.
On summer days, on summer days
It's so lovely and hot, so come out to play.

Katie Buchanan (9)
Burham CE Primary School, Rochester

In Praise Of Summer

We love summer,
The ice cream,
The sun's beam,
The Kent cricket team.

We could burn in this sun,
But we still have fun,
We can sunbathe.

We can have more fruit,
Strawberries are yummy,
I got lots in my tummy.

I love to swim,
Not when the sky's dim,
I play with Tim.

A water fight is good,
Don't wear a hood,
You will get soaked.

Go to the beach for the day,
Near the bay,
Get a friend to play.

Nathan Hudson (9)
Burham CE Primary School, Rochester

In Praise Of Summer

Summer is great, you can play with your mates,
Summer is fun, you can play chase,
Summer is great, you can have water fights,
Summer is beautiful because of the flowers,
Summer is delightful because of the bugs,
Summer is enjoyable because of the weather,
Summer is wonderful, you can sit by the lake.

Charlotte Moore (8)
Burham CE Primary School, Rochester

In Praise Of Summer

Sand is with beaches
We go once a day
And it will be a lovely day.

We love ice creams
We have it twice a day
It melts down your fingers
And then down your toes.

We love swimming pools
And paddling pools too
We swim about
We splash about
And then we shout, 'Wahoo'.

I think the sun is wonderful
Do you like the sun too?
I like to shout out loud,
Do you too?
I have great might
And I can see a wonderful sight.

Bethany Cownden (9)
Burham CE Primary School, Rochester

In Praise Of Summer

Summer, summer, we play outside
Summer, summer, the sun never dies
Summer, summer, we go to the beach.

Summer, summer, I love cold drinks
Summer, summer, you're the best
Summer, summer, better than the rest.

Summer, summer, you're the best season of all
Summer, summer, I love you all
Summer, summer, you could be my mate.

David Mills (8)
Burham CE Primary School, Rochester

In Praise Of Summer

In summer I am going to France,
I can't eat the snails because they'll put me in a trance,
I'll take my own food,
So I don't have to eat frogs' legs too!

Summer is fun, do you like it too?
Don't tell me, let me guess
I think the answer might just be yes!
Summer is the best season of all!

I hate it when it thunders
The lightning's horrible, it makes power cuts
Thunderstorms are terrible
I love the sun, you can go outside
Summer is the best!

Winter's worst, then comes autumn
Spring is second best
But I like summer best of all.

Beatrice Syer (7)
Burham CE Primary School, Rochester

In Praise Of Summer

I love the sun yes I do
I wonder if you do too?
You get covered up by cloud
Then you start to shout out loud
You're more powerful than rain
Strength is what you gain
You are so bright
And you have great might
You let us with joy scream
And you let us eat ice cream
I love the sun yes I do
I wonder if you do too?

Simon Treays (9)
Burham CE Primary School, Rochester

In Praise Of Summer

Summer is great
Summer is cool
Summer is a pool
With a ball

We have ice poles
We have ice creams
We have ice lollies
With the sun

It doesn't rain much
It is a pain
When it rains again
On a sunny day

In summer
We get sprayed
With a hose
Under trees
We like the shade.

Jordan Field (9)
Burham CE Primary School, Rochester

In Praise Of Summer

We are going on holiday,
I am ready for a trip,
I had to wake up at 4 today,
Now I am in the aeroplane I can have a kip.

Now we are having fun,
Splashing in the clear pool,
With the shining sun,
We have a fan that keeps us cool.

Summer you have come to the end,
I hope you come back again,
You drive me round the bend,
Please come back again.

Chloe Strachan (9)
Burham CE Primary School, Rochester

In Praise Of Summer

Summer, summer,
You are the best
Summer, summer
We love you

Summer, summer
You grow trees
Summer, summer
You are hot and
You have a breeze

Summer, summer
You are the one
Summer, summer
We splash in the pool

Summer, summer
You can run
Summer, summer
You have fun

Summer, summer
You have to come
To the end
Summer, summer
And come back again.

Chloe Trustam (9)
Burham CE Primary School, Rochester

In Praise Of Summer

Summer is brilliant,
We have wonderful ice creams,
Birds singing,
And we have the sunshine.

Summer we like,
Winter we dislike,
There is no snow in summer,
But there is snow in winter.

Summer is cool
Because we play in our pools,
We play out more,
When it is sunny.

Summer is hot
Because of the sun,
We enjoy this season,
We like the others.

Summer is enjoyable
When you sit in the shade,
It is alive,
When you sit in the sunshine.

Andrew Grierson (9)
Burham CE Primary School, Rochester

In Praise Of Summer

In the summer
The ice cream van comes,
To give you an ice cream
To cool you down.

In the summer,
Plants grow,
Really well,
Some of them have a lovely scent.

In the summer,
You can go to the beach
To sunbathe for a day,
So you get a tan.

In the summer,
You can have a water fight
And get very wet,
So then
you can dry off in the sun.

In the summer,
It is fine,
And I will be nine,
Have a wonderful time.

Callum Gibson (8)
Burham CE Primary School, Rochester

Easter

E aster means love and peace
A t home and in school
S niffing all the carrots
T he Easter bunny comes
E ating all the Easter eggs
R unning round about.

Xana Brites De Campos (9)
European School, Italy

The School Teacher

She's big and fat,
She looks like a rat.

She's the big ugly boss
And she's always so cross.

She's the school teacher
And sometimes I hate her.

Although she's quite kind,
She muddles my mind.

She's as fast as lightning,
And sometimes she's frightening.

I'm quite good in class,
In spelling tests I pass.

I love maths
And I practise when I have baths.

When I'm at home I groan
And always moan.

Noemi Perujo Holland (9)
European School, Italy

Mathematics

M y favourite lesson is maths
A nd all the things with that
T he best in the world
H ave no other word
E ven or odd
M aths is a god
A nd the best thing is
T he number counting
I love maths
C an you believe that?

Balint Wirnhardt (10)
European School, Italy

The Magic Girl

There once was a magic girl,
Who travelled around the world,
She once met a cat who stole her hat,
There once was a magic girl.

There once was a magic girl,
Who flew around the world,
She once met a frog who was quite a hog,
There once was a magic girl.

There once was a magic girl,
Who walked around the world,
She once met a dog who jumped a log,
There once was a magic girl.

There once was a magic girl,
Who drove around the world,
She once met a boy who had a nice toy
And they became friends.

Julia Laitinen (9)
European School, Italy

Winter Icicles

W hat a surprise
I cicles hanging from roofs
N o noises
T ransparent diamonds
E legant pictures
R eflecting light

I cicles big and small
C linging when they break
I cicles so beautiful
C ouldn't they stay always
L aying broken on the ground
E njoyment's over
S lowly fading away.

Riccardo Bica (10)
European School, Italy

Cuddly But Smelly

They are cuddly and warm
    friendly and loving
They are our friends
    and mine is named George

From time to time he smells
    he is not just stinky but also dinky
He leaves hair and marks wherever he goes
    but does not go willingly in the bath
but willingly plays in the paddling pool

His slaves are awful, they fly through the room
    the dribbling is not much better, it hangs down
He needs to use mouthwash
    but like his kisses I still do

He is my best friend and I got him for Christmas
    but I hate cleaning up after him, especially the poo
He shares my cuddly toys and also my food
    have you guessed who he is?
He is my dog, George.

Harry Starost (9)
European School, Italy

Logic Gates

L ogic gates, ones and zeros
O utput changes
G ates control
I nput zeros and ones
C ontrol the computer

G ates And, Or, Not
A nd is probably zero
T ransforming zeros and ones
E xit is called output
S witching off.

Jacob Bloodworth (9)
European School, Italy

I Always Wanted A Pet . . . Dragon!

I always wanted a pet dragon
It would be very fun,
To have a reptile in the house,
(Without disturbing Mum)

I'd play with it all day,
I'd take it out for walks
And if I'd teach it English,
People would then shout, 'It talks!'

It would turn my enemies to dust,
He'd come with me to school
And all the students in my class,
Would think he's very cool!

People wouldn't be scared of him,
'Cause he wouldn't only like me,
One day I'll have a dragon,
Just you wait and see!

Maria Vakali (9)
European School, Italy

Carnival

C ostumes everywhere in shops,
A s many as you can imagine,
R unning children with their money,
N o one forgets to buy one,
I n the streets the procession has already begun,
V ampires, cowboys, fairies, butterflies, kings and queens,
A ll shouting, dancing and singing,
L et's celebrate! It's Carnival!

Catarina Fattori Melo Amaral (9)
European School, Italy

The Tiger

The tiger creeps slowly in the night,
Hoping that she might,
Catch a little animal to eat.
She finds a little rabbit hopping on its own,
In a clear, wide, peaceful zone.
The tiger crouches, pounces, attacks and claws
The poor little thing and takes it by the neck to her cave
And there in the cave her cubs await
For their mother to arrive with their prey
And when their mother arrives, they all come alive
And say to their food, 'Yum-yum.'

Tara Das (9)
European School, Italy

Leah

Leah is a girl
A pretty girl at that
She has nice long blonde hair
It looks lovely in a plait
Her mother has three sons
They're Adam, Saul and Oren
Leah's by herself
Except for her nice mother, Susan
Leah is so pretty
She likes Hello Kitty
And guess what she is . . .
She is my best friend!

Shona Cosgrove (9)
European School, Italy

Mum's Old Car For Sale

My mum's old car
Is now for sale,
She drove so far,
She turned all pale,
So Mum decided to put her on sale.

She's now so tired
Of those long trips,
So sometimes she turns all quiet,
Quite often she needs a mechanic's flips,
So now Mum's really put her on sale.

She's though still in shape
And would hate to get wrecked
And I'm sure her heart would break,
Should her body already be cracked,
'So therefore,' says Mum, 'she is for sale.'

Poor Mum's old car - there is no cure,
I really hope she'll get sold,
I'll miss her for sure,
But my heart won't go cold,
I'll keep warm in my mum's
Brand new car!

Martin Skejo-Andresen (9)
European School, Italy

Spring Is Coming

Spring is coming and it is getting hotter
Flowers are beginning to blossom
People are wearing lighter clothes
The days are getting longer
All the snow is melting and the fruits are growing!

Naomi Tawiah (9)
European School, Italy

The River

The river is quiet,
Quiet as a mouse,
Slinking down the hill,
The deepest hill.

It is blue like the sky,
It glitters when it goes through the bends,
It jumps over a stone,
Hides under a branch,
The river is quiet,
Quiet as a mouse.

Sofia Nyman (9)
European School, Italy

The Deep Blue Sea

The deep blue sea,
Wider than a river,
Bluer than a stream.

The water's glistening,
As the sun's reflection shines down,
Even when the sun is setting,
The waves will still ripple.

Very softly the fish swim by,
Occasionally the dolphins swim to the surface,
Whales, fish, dolphins and coral,
When the sun burns brightly,
People go to swim in the deep blue sea!

Louisa Tagziria (10)
European School, Italy

Shannon Berry

Shannon is a little girl,
With long blonde hair and not much curl,
She's got bright blue eyes and a button nose,
With freckles all the way down to her toes.

Her mum is from Scotland,
Her dad is from Wales,
She's got four big brothers,
Who always tell tales.

She was born in Lugano,
At a quarter to three,
You've guessed who that girl is,
Yes, Shannon is me.

Shannon Berry (9)
European School, Italy

The Horse

Some are wild and some are tame,
Some are fast and swift,
Some are violent,
Some are kind, but still,
I love you all the same.

You are clever,
You are strong,
You have power over everyone.

Sigrid Huld (9)
European School, Italy

The Mermaids

On the beach watching the dolphins jumping out of the wavy water.
Moonbeams bouncing on her shiny tail.
Hair as cold as Pluto.
Diving from the rocks into the sapphire-blue sea.
Singing with the quiet sea otters.
Looking at Boot Strap Bill's sunken treasure chest
Wide open with the gold medallion sitting in the skull.

James Boxall (8)
Fetlar Primary School, Shetland

I Saw A Mermaid

Sitting on the rocks with a butterfly clip in her hair,
Brushing it with a shell.

Watching dolphins, with her hair drooped over the side.

Her tail purple and blue.

Exciting shades glittering in the sun.

Hair as gold as the sun.

Playing with the dolphins in the shiny, sapphire-blue sea.

Whispering in a cave with three sea horses
And a sea turtle so that the shark outside didn't hear.

I saw a mermaid under the deep, deep blue sapphire sea,
Gazing at the sunken ship.

Dazzled, for they had found a treasure chest.

Rowan Boxall (10)
Fetlar Primary School, Shetland

Green Tails

One mermaid lying on the hot
sand eating a big fat fish

Two mermaids with shiny green
tails sparkling in the sun

Three mermaids with hair as
shiny as the sun

Four mermaids playing and
splashing in the dark blue water

Five mermaids booming happily
at the friendly killer whales

Six mermaids under the glittering water
staring at the sparkling white starfish inside a rotting brown boat.

Tom Thomason (7)
Fetlar Primary School, Shetland

Six Mermaids

One mermaid on the rocks
Sunbathing with her tail on the sand below.

Two mermaids with scaly glowing tails in the sun.

Three mermaids with hair as glittery as the sun.

Four mermaids playing at catching the starfish.

Five mermaids giggling in a cave
With sea otters and making 200 jokes.

Six mermaids staring at six starfish in a line,

Nine walrus going home

And four sea otters
Playing with a beach ball.

Frank Coutts (9)
Fetlar Primary School, Shetland

Life's Decision

I've just been born,
Under the heat
And now I've got
The world at my feet.
What should I do
When I'm older?
I could be a shareholder,
No, that won't do!
Years later I wonder,
Still stuck what to do,
Wait! I know!
I skill with Will,
So I join the army,
Free the world of evil!
Now I'm where I want to be,
Now everyone can see,
That I fight for me,
I rid the world of evil,
Not one bad soul can dwell!
Now I've come to the end of my life,
So brothers, farewell!

Daniel Sheppard (9)
Gig Mill Primary School, Stourbridge

If I Win The Lottery

When I get older, I want to win the lottery,
Then what would I do?
I'd have a big house,
With a big wardrobe
With millions of dresses inside,
I'd have many little places to hide away,
Where nobody would find me
And I'd have a big lounge
Where I could sit in peace.

Laura-Beth Green (9)
Gig Mill Primary School, Stourbridge

Can't Choose

I can't choose what to be
For when I get older,
Maybe a sailor at sea,
But then, what about scurvy?

Cool, I could be a spy,
Yeah, I'm rather sneaky.
I'll work for the FBI!
But what if I get caught?

Maybe I'll be a vet!
I'm okay with blood
And I've already got a pet,
But what about dead pets?

I'll have to leave it another day,
To choose what I could be.
There's no other way,
Let's hope it comes to me . . .

Sarah Bayliss (9)
Gig Mill Primary School, Stourbridge

Being A Star

I would like to be a star,
I would like to go really far.

Have lots of fans,
Hire a cook to deal with all those pots and pans.

I would like to be one of the riches,
Be in all those pictures.

I would like to have my name on everything,
That's some of the things the life of a star can bring.

Kathryn Hedar (9)
Gig Mill Primary School, Stourbridge

My Dream

I dream of singing on a stage
Being the best pop star
Dancing around, cheering I hear

Walking through my mansion
Miles it must be
A room of money, jewels, diamonds

My wardrobe's as big as an elephant's pen
Clothes sparkling all around
Jeans, greatest in the world
I am the best

Going to Hollywood
Greece, Spain, Canada
Poshest hotels
I walk down the aisle greeted by the Queen
Sit to have a chat

Bright lights in my eyes
Oh it was a dream!

Jessica Watson (10)
Gig Mill Primary School, Stourbridge

The World At Our Feet

The limo pulls up,
The red carpet goes down,
As the door opens a crowd gathers round,
Flashing lights here and there,
As I walk up the aisle in a fair velvet dress.

There is a premier of my big movie,
I sit and watch it
And I think,
Is that me?

Sophie Siviter (9)
Gig Mill Primary School, Stourbridge

My Dream

I was once a baby,
As cute as can be,
I was always sitting on my father's knee,
'You've got the world at your feet,' he'd always say,
Each and every single day.
When I got older, I'd say,
It was a great day at school,
Except they called me a fool for dreaming today,
I wanted to be a traveller,
Sail the seven seas,
Go to the Caribbean
Or heal the Japanese,
I went to another school
And they called me a fool,
For wanting to dream today.

Shelby Cartwright (10)
Gig Mill Primary School, Stourbridge

Upon The Waves

You sail along,
Waves are bobbing,
Up and down you go,
On a seasick ship,
Not far left to go.

'Ahoy me mates,'
Shouts the captain aloud,
I see land ahead
And the fluffy clouds.

The sails are up,
As we drift along,
Landing on a
Desert island!

Alison Horton (9)
Gig Mill Primary School, Stourbridge

My Dream

When I'm older, I want to play for Villa
Me and my friend George Caterpillar
When I play for Villa, Birmingham City will be dead
And poor Robbie Savage will be old and lying in bed
The FA Premier League we will win
And then we will make a humongous din
Then I wake up from my dream
I'll go downstairs and have some strawberries and cream
In the lounge are my mum and dad
If they see me they'll be mad.

Jacob Gledhill (9)
Gig Mill Primary School, Stourbridge

Football Star

I want to play for Liverpool one day,
Be the best player in the world,
Have loads of money and a great big mansion,
I would score a hat-trick every week,
Have a Ferrari and a Lamborghini
And a pool all for me,
Also have a go-kart track and race my son every day,
But I won't play unless they pay,
That is my dream for when I am older
And I hope to score every day.

Callum Scott (9)
Gig Mill Primary School, Stourbridge

I Want To Play

I want to play for Wolves one day,
But I know it will not happen,
If it did, I'd shout hooray and run off up to play,
Be the best in the whole world and score every day,
It's time to play, the ball comes to me, I shoot, I score.

Matthew Jones (9)
Gig Mill Primary School, Stourbridge

The Big Game
(Manchester United Vs Wolves)

It was a massive crowd
And it was really loud
But I was proud
We came out onto the pitch
I saw their injured player who had a stitch
And then I felt an itch
People were roaring
And it was a little pouring
And the game got a little boring
Until they scored
And all the crowd roared
But I knew the game wasn't over yet.

Jack Stanier (9)
Gig Mill Primary School, Stourbridge

Can You Choose One For Me?

Look at me, what shall I be?
Maybe a footballer,
Maybe a star,
Maybe I could play an electric guitar,
What about an explorer
Or an animal carer too,
It is I say entirely up to you,
Shall I be a therapist
Or maybe a writer,
Then I will probably be brighter!
These are the things I want to be,
Can you choose one
Just for me?

Zoë Emery (9)
Gig Mill Primary School, Stourbridge

Somewhere In Time

In that room over there,
I am sitting in a chair,
I look up to the sky,
My desire in my eyes,
I counted 1, 2, 3
And said, 'I just want to be
A scientist.'

In my room upstairs,
I have loads and loads of hardware,
After school, every day,
I go up to my mum and say,
'I will be a scientist someday,
Just give me a chance,
Just give me some time,
I will be a scientist,
Somewhere in time.'

William Harding (9)
Gig Mill Primary School, Stourbridge

My Car

When I grow older, I'm going to buy a car,
But not just any, I'm going to buy a Mazarati
With gleaming alloys and sparkling panels,
Like a lake flashing in the sun or . . .
No, I think I'd prefer a TVR, oh, what a car,
Or maybe a Lexus, Bentley, Aston Martin
Or even a kit car spartin.

Matt Pugh (9)
Gig Mill Primary School, Stourbridge

My Dream Ferrari

My Ferrari is bright and red
Yes, that's right it's the colour of blood
It never gets covered in mud
No, not one speck at all

My Ferrari is the best
The fastest of them all
And when I go to bed
I triple lock the garage door

It hasn't got a dent
Not even a single scratch
A Lamborghini isn't a match
Because my Ferrari is smarter than that

My Ferrari is the best
And you can't get better than that.

Kieren Pratty (9)
Gig Mill Primary School, Stourbridge

Ferrari

To ride a Ferrari is my dream
To ride it up and down the stream
Passing over the frozen lake
Might even run over a snake

It looks like it hasn't got a scratch
If I entered a competition nothing would be a match
I just really love the way it zooms
Go too fast and it booms
It picks up speed every second
Until it goes out of sight
Zooooom.

Daniel Gilson (9)
Gig Mill Primary School, Stourbridge

Wet Rain

Rain spreads elegantly like a graceful swan dancing through the night,
She drops from Heaven with her cold freezing wings,
She takes over all the world with her transparent look.

Storm proposed to her, she walks down the aisle with her cold wet face,
Her veil is being lifted up, the world is free now.

On a cold, wet night Rain falls into the water and dies in
                                        her slumbersome sleep.

Tiyah Hernandez (8)
Hampden Gurney Primary School, London

Silence Listens

It was so quiet that
I heard the children blinking

It was so quiet that
I heard someone walking

It was so quiet that
I heard my sister eating

It was so quiet that
I heard leaves dripping

It was so quiet that
I heard owls speaking

It was so quiet that
I heard the sun come up

It was so quiet that
I heard people walking on carpet

It was so quiet that
I heard people tiptoeing.

Renna Kassir (8)
Hampden Gurney Primary School, London

The Lightning Poem

Light the glistening lightning always is bright,
If you go under him you will be struck by the light.
His might will strike,
Only if you use your bike,
Sneakily he flies and cries,
Just when he misses his prey.

Ashes off the trees,
Seem to trash the whole city,
He sits in the air with the whole world stinky.

Day by day he calms down,
All the best for the whole town.

Chioke Morgan Brown (9)
Hampden Gurney Primary School, London

Moon

She pulled back the starry light,
Balls of silver hanging in the sky,
She is bright and high.

The moon shines a lot at night
And gives us the darkness of might,
The sun and moon fight all day,
'You'd better do this or you'll pay,'
As the sun runs away, the moon goes to play.

Paula and Israa go to the moon
And ask, 'Where is the darkness?
Some people need to go to sleep you know.

When are you going to make the night old might?'

Paula Otalvora (9)
Hampden Gurney Primary School, London

Silver Moon

The moon yawned and slowly opened his eyes,
He pulled back the white clouds,
The Earth was shining white,
Everyone was sleeping in bed,
Everything looked dark and spooky,
When the sun came the silver moon went to sleep in
His soft and comfortable sky.

Abdullah Puri (8)
Hampden Gurney Primary School, London

Moon Shining

She got up at night
And shone so bright
You cannot look at the bright light
Because she shines so bright.

Everybody does not know what she looks like
Because she shines so bright
And can blind you with her light
Do you know who she looks like?
Everyone does not see her face
For she is the shadow and she is the place.

Noir El-Nour (8)
Hampden Gurney Primary School, London

Powerful Lightning

The powerful lightning goes through the night
Supersonic with his partner, Thunder
They go through the sky together scaring the world
He breaks down everything with his powerful body
Nothing can stop him and on a rainy day he walks through the night.

Richard Lewis (8)
Hampden Gurney Primary School, London

Silence Listens

It was so quiet that I could hear the children blinking.
It was so quiet that I could hear the washing drying.
It was so quiet that I could hear the leaves falling down.
It was so quiet that I could hear the sun coming up.
It was so quiet that I could hear my brother eating.

Olivia Curtis (9)
Hampden Gurney Primary School, London

The Moon Is Shining

The moon awakes from her deep sleep
And pulls away the shiny star curtains
Oh moon, she thought, *what will the world do with me*
And the shiny star curtains?
The moon came out and battered the world
With her silver rays.

Faisal Piracha (9)
Hampden Gurney Primary School, London

Deadly Tornado

The tornado is always scaring you,
Everywhere you go you always will know
On a hot day he stamps all the way
As he smashes at the windows across
The world with the light
Then at night you start to get a fright.

Kieran George (9)
Hampden Gurney Primary School, London

Light Moon

When the moon is full
And high in the sky,
Wolves come out to play,
We look at the sky,
What do we see?
I see a yellow banana,
We peel back the skin
And the skin looks white and light.

The moon is soft,
Child: Oh moon, moody one,
You are the lightest moon in the world,
Goodnight moon,
Shh, the moon is a sleeping moon: *zzzzz!*

Baatar Sod-Uyanga (9)
Hampden Gurney Primary School, London

The Queen Of Snow

The crispy snow falls to Earth
Spreading her babies everywhere she goes
If you stare for a long time you'll notice her glow
Every minute she lays at least 20,000 eggs
You might not know this
But snow doesn't like us but we like her
When the sad moment comes to say goodbye
She melts to the floor
Will we meet again?

Israa Fawaz (9)
Hampden Gurney Primary School, London

The Wolf Shining

The moon is full and high in the sky
The werewolf comes out to play
The wolf comes out to eat your bed sheets

The moon's darkness quietens the night
When everyone is fast asleep

The sun comes up, the moon goes down
The wolf runs away to get some sleep.

Aaron Brown (9)
Hampden Gurney Primary School, London

Amanda

Amanda,
Cute, great
Teaching, chatting, helping
Brown hair, skin colour, blue eyes, red lips,
Teacher.

Shreeda Mehta (8)
Hampden Gurney Primary School, London

Moon

While shining Moon comes out to play,
Who scared all the stars away?
She played with all the cheerful children
With her little balls of cheese
The white world turned into snow
Furious Moon shut dark clouds away
Oh Moon, bad-tempered one,
How can we sleep without you, Moon?

Charlotte Kerr (9)
Hampden Gurney Primary School, London

My Friend

Shreeda
Warm, beautiful
Swimming, swinging, climbing
Loyal, best friend is excellent
Kind, bright,
Shreeda.

Zoe Pahne (8)
Hampden Gurney Primary School, London

Me!

Jumana
Confident, beautiful
Swimming, catching, throwing
Jumana likes catching and throwing
Jumana

Ismail
Confident, good
Swimming, having fun, playing
Ismail likes everyone
Jumana.

Jumana Ismail (7)
Hampden Gurney Primary School, London

My Friend

Joe
Good, normal
Likes golf, swimming, climbing
Fast, friendly, polite, respectful,
Charlie.

Joseph Howe (7)
Hampden Gurney Primary School, London

Secret Agent

Agent 6A
Smart, gadgety, active
Climbing, jumping high, parachuting
Full of fun, fantastic, powerful
DN Agent.

Andrew Mitrousis (7)
Hampden Gurney Primary School, London

Friend

S oft as a bunny
A ctive and cuddly
R elaxing in the sun
A ctive and warm
H appy and funny
    what a good friend!

Bonnie Heaton (7)
Hampden Gurney Primary School, London

My Friend

Alim
Short but is fast
Kicking, throwing, running
Fast when playing around
Charlie.

Gela Karumidze (7)
Hampden Gurney Primary School, London

My Friend

Kiah
Funny, clever
Dance, bounce, catch
Ginger, white, green big
Great.

Megan Elie (8)
Hampden Gurney Primary School, London

Seaside

S ailing out on the beach,
E ating a nice juicy peach,
A nice big wave comes sailing in,
S aw a dolphin and its fin,
I came back onto the sand,
D reaming, dozing on the land,
E ating a doughnut, listening to a band.

Taylor Green (8)
Hampden Gurney Primary School, London

Snow

Snow
Freezing, fun
Comes, melts, drips
It drips in the heat
Ice.

Stefan Svrdlin (8)
Hampden Gurney Primary School, London

My Friend - Cinquain

Megan,
Kind, generous
Caring, helpful, funny
Playful with others, has brown eyes
Is fun.

Ryan Welan (8)
Hampden Gurney Primary School, London

Kilburn Acrostic Poem

K nowing all the people,
I n the morning,
L ike in the sunshine,
B usy in the traffic,
U p on the high road,
R unning on the street,
N owhere to go.

Khamarl Christie (8)
Hampden Gurney Primary School, London

Bicycle

Bike
Fast, fun
Speedy, powerful object
Two wheels, one seat vehicle
Excellent.

Charlie Bishton-Worley (8)
Hampden Gurney Primary School, London

Snowman

Snowman
Wet, cold
Big, fluffy, sad
Walking in the sun, melting
Lonely.

Bahareh Nassiri (8)
Hampden Gurney Primary School, London

Birds In The Sky

Swifts move swiftly through the rocks
And hens are looking for the cockerels,
While eagles fly with their great eyes.
The falcons are having their fly.
The coal tits are having a marvellous time
And the blue tits fly past the line.
Crows are scaring a scarecrow
And the seagulls are flying low.
Robins are having their winter,
But the blackbirds have a splinter.
Doves are always flying with leaves
And the magpies are little thieves.
The sparrows are coming through your door
And the thrushes are breaking the law.

Georgia Harding (9)
Iwade Community Primary School, Kent

If I Was A Ruler

If I was a ruler,
I'd be put on a paper,
I'd be a long rectangle,
Helping to draw a line.

If I was a ruler,
I'd be writing a song,
I would listen to the music
And I'll be singing along.

If I was a ruler,
I'd measure a house,
I'd measure another one
And I would measure a mouse.

Kieran Smith (8)
Iwade Community Primary School, Kent

If I Were A Shape

If I were a square
I'd be a window looking over the world
If I were a circle
I'd be a clock telling the time
If I were a cube
I'd be multilink in a numeracy lesson
If I were a shape.

Ben Williams (7)
Iwade Community Primary School, Kent

Jack And The Beanstalk

Once upon a day,
A little boy called Jack would play.
His mum would work on the farm all day,
But there wasn't enough pay.
He gave the money to his mum,
But it turned out to be some hay.

She threw it out the window,
But next day it became a pea.
Then, the pea became a tree.
So Jack climbed the tree to the clouds,
He popped up his head
And he saw ahead,
A castle guarded by a marshal.

The giant was asleep,
So Jack had a peep.
Suddenly, a roar rumbled the floor,
'Fi! Fie! Fo! Fum!' shouted the giant's tum,
Jack darted back down the stalk's beaten track,
Then shouted, 'Mum, get the axe!'

Simon Lawrence (9)
Iwade Community Primary School, Kent

Jack

There once was a boy called Jack
Who wanted to sleep in a sack
He slept with a dummy
Mum said, 'It ain't funny,
Because the coalman wants it back!'

Jack Cooper (11)
Iwade Community Primary School, Kent

The Three Little Pigs

One day there were three little pigs,
One was small, one was big,
One was called Ryan Giggs.

One of the pigs made a house,
Made out of straw, that little louse!

As the wolf came over,
In his brand new Rover,
He said, 'Can I come in?'
The pigs replied, 'No, not by the point of my pinny pin pin!'
So the wolf came in,
With a big bin
And ate the pig!

As this happened, the pigs
Knew this so they pulled their twigs
And shot the wolf,
Those little kids!

Matthew Putnam (9)
Iwade Community Primary School, Kent

In Daniel's Room He Kept

In Daniel's room he kept . . .
10 fat pigs,
9 nosy owls,
8 stinky rats,
7 hungry dogs,
6 lazy cats,
5 crazy monkeys,
4 large hippos,
3 fierce spiders,
2 squeaky mice,
1 great elephant
And a big noisy room of animals.

Daniel Easton (8)
Iwade Community Primary School, Kent

A School Bag

There was a bag, an icky, sticky, old smelly, school bag with . . .
10 broken pencil cases
9 old pieces of shoelaces
8 pinky sticky bubblegums
7 pieces of paper of maths sums
6 little, bouncy, red balls
5 small and big toy tools
4 packs of old torn card games
3 tiny bugs who don't know their names
2 old soggy choco bars, er, er, yummy
And 1 small mouse said, 'I want my mummy.'

Adam Cox (8)
Iwade Community Primary School, Kent

My Classroom

I'm living in a classroom,
I've been there all my life,
But now I'm moving somewhere else,
It really is quite nice,
I loved it in my old classroom,
I'm very scared of moving,
Just take a deep breath
And see how it goes,
It can be quite nice,
Or can be quite scary,
I really don't mind.

Zoe Whiffen (8)
Iwade Community Primary School, Kent

Shape Poem

If I was a rectangle
I would be a door with a shining handle
If I was a rectangle
I'd be a table with some work on top
I'd be a window to see far away
I'd be a whiteboard with writing on me
I'd be a book you can never finish
If I was a rectangle.

Conner Millington (8)
Iwade Community Primary School, Kent

The Crocodile

A crocodile is green
A crocodile is big
It makes a lumble jumble sound
And goes snap, snap, snap
And has humongous white teeth.

Ellie Cooper (7)
Iwade Community Primary School, Kent

Hamsters

Scuttling creatures,
Rustling creatures,
They have the most amazing features,
Running around,
Along the ground,
Sniffing anything that they've found,
Rustling creatures,
Scuttling creatures,
Hamsters have the most amazing features.

Jasmin Kisnorbo (9)
Iwade Community Primary School, Kent

In Casey's Bedroom, Casey Kept . . .

In Casey's bedroom, Casey kept . . .
10 stripy zebras running about,
9 blackbirds that pecked the floor,
8 slithery snakes slithering on the green grass,
7 white cats chasing the mice,
6 mice eating cheese,
5 brown dogs barking at the cats,
4 blue fish swimming in a tank,
3 woolly sheep being lazy all day,
2 lazy pigs being lazy all day
And 1 elephant who couldn't fit in the bedroom.

Casey Stone (8)
Iwade Community Primary School, Kent

Friendship

F riends are good to have,
R eal friends are never bad,
I n hard times they are always there,
E very time they care,
N o matter how hard things get,
D own to the deepest depths,
S tanding by your side,
H elping you to survive,
I' m glad they are there,
P erhaps we can all learn to share.

Charlotte Mills (9)
Iwade Community Primary School, Kent

One By One

One by one
One by one
Monkeys saying this is fun
Two by two
Two by two
Monsters bursting for the loo
Three by three
Three by three
Penguins dancing in the sea
Four by four
Four by four
Spiders crawling on the floor
Five by five
Five by five
Whales going for a dive
Six by six
Six by six
Builders desperate for a fix
Seven by seven
Seven by seven
Whales laughing in blue heaven
Eight by eight
Eight by eight
Children climbing on my gate
Nine by nine
Nine by nine
Baby saying I'm fine
Ten by ten
Ten by ten
Dogs after lazy hens.

David Easton (8)
Iwade Community Primary School, Kent

Little Red Riding Hood

Once upon a time in the neighbourhood,
There was a girl who was ever so good.
She went to her granny's house one day,
This time she went the long way.

A wolf came strolling by and took a short cut,
You'll never guess where, Granny's hut!

When the wolf got there he ate a pear
And said, 'That's not enough!' therefore ate Granny, bare!

Red Riding Hood entered just then and yelled,
'I'm coming up with a frying pan,
Be careful 'cause here I am!
Oh Grandma! why have you got lots of hair?
And, plus, why are you sitting in a chair?

Grandma, look at your eye!
I think I'd better say goodbye.'

Somebody's ringing the bell, *ding-dong!*
I think the guy outside's singing a song.
It was a wolf that chased her up and down the stairs,
She hit him with some of Granny's chairs!

There was a knock at the door,
Which revealed the woodcutter
And in his hand he had a putter!

He whacked the wolf's belly,
Which when opened, was very smelly.
The wolf got sent to Dover,
Where he bought himself
A brand new Rover!

Manny Latunde (9)
Iwade Community Primary School, Kent

School

S chool is a fantastic place so some say,
C hildren like fun lessons and going out to play,
H istory can be OK if you're in a right mood,
O f course some say you want food,
O ver the hills and far away stands another school on a beautiful day,
L ovely hot day in May.

Emily Fitton (9)
Iwade Community Primary School, Kent

The Three Little Pigs

Three little pigs made a house of sticks
And two more of straw and bricks.
One fine day a wolf came along,
Big and bad he ponged, what a bong.
Wolf yelled, 'Let me in or I'll steal your straw!'
Pig one cried, 'But could you leave my door?'
Pull, pull, pull, snap!
That pig had his final nap.
Wolf called, 'I'll snap your twigs and come right in.'
Pig two asked, 'Could you leave my chin?'
The wolf strolled to pig three,
Oh golly gosh, oh deary me.
Wolf yelled, 'I'm getting my bazooka!'
Pig three called, 'What! A carooka?'
Bang!
That didn't hurt the walls, that old wolf
Gave up and now plays golf.

Warren James (10)
Iwade Community Primary School, Kent

The Three Little Pigs

Three little pigs went for a walk,
Went for a walk, went for a walk,
Three little pigs went for a walk,
One summer's day.

Bricks and straw and skinny sticks,
They made their houses so very quick.

The big bad wolf came along,
Came along, came along,
The big bad wolf came along,
One summer's day.

The big bad wolf blew the straw down,
Blew the straw down, blew the straw down,
The big bad wolf blew the straw down,
One summer's day.

The weak stick house was no longer up,
No longer up, no longer up,
The weak stick house was no longer up,
One summer's day.

The strong brick house was always up,
Always up, always up,
The strong brick house was always up,
One summer's day.

Connor Edis (10)
Iwade Community Primary School, Kent

Jack And The Beanstalk

Once there was a boy called Jack,
who lived with his brother called Zack.
He needed money, can't you see,
so he sold his poor cow, Daisy.

In return he got a bean,
from the man who was never seen.
In a flash Jack raced back home,
where his mother gave a terrible groan.

'You silly boy!' his mother moaned,
'You sold my cow,' old Mum frowned.
'Sorry Mum, but just take a peek.'
'OK, OK, I'll go and see.'

Mum leaned over and took a look,
'It's horrible,' she shook.
Mum snatched it out of poor Jack's hand
and threw it out into the sand.

Jack ran out and looked around,
but nothing was small and round.
He looked up and there he saw,
a big green stem a hundred feet tall.

'Hello,' said the beanstalk,
'Please don't talk.'
'You can't,' said Jack, 'you're just a stalk.'
'I can, it's true, I can speak, I can make you have a beat.
Please climb up and take a look,
you will see a very big person, she is a cook.'

So Jack climbed up and peered right through
and saw a giant who saw Jack,
gobbled him up in a sack.

Nowadays people still believe
Jack's still alive and he still breathes.
Most people think it's funny,
but Jack's in the giant's tummy.

Shaina Ormston (9)
Iwade Community Primary School, Kent

Goldilocks And The Three Bears

On one fine summer's day
Three bears went out to play,
Their porridge was so very hot,
Back at the house Goldi ate from a pot.
Next she sat down on a chair,
After she made a mess everywhere.
So she went for a lie down,
The bears came home and gave a frown,
Goldilocks is now in jail,
Receiving quite a lot of mail!

Jack Anderson (10)
Iwade Community Primary School, Kent

Three Little Pigs And The Big Bad Wolf

There was once a wolf, which ate a cork,
Ever since that day,
He ate everything that got in his way.
Then he came across
A little house that was nearly moss,
But then he saw it was straw.

He went to give it a little kick,
But then he saw it belonged to a pig.
He shouted through the letter box,
'To eat you up I will get a fox
And put it through the letter box.'

The pig said, 'No you won't.'
'I'll blow the house down,'
The wolf said with a frown.
That's exactly what he did,
Then ate the pig
And that's the last thing he ever did.

Daniel Elliott (9)
Iwade Community Primary School, Kent

Titanic

Big and bold
  Titanium gold
Ten thousand passengers
  Young and old
Two lovers aboard
  Sharing the Lord

Big and bold
  Titanium gold
Waiting to be sunk
  With a big dunk
Rich and poor
  Waiting at the captain's door.

Jack Ince (10) & Jack Fitton (11)
Iwade Community Primary School, Kent

Sorry

I care for you,
You don't for me,
At least as friends,
We still can be,
I am so sorry,
Forgive me please,
Here I am,
On bended knees,
A friend like you,
I would not lose,
So time I give,
Your mind to choose.

Sophie Carmody (11)
Iwade Community Primary School, Kent

Rules

Pay attention
Or get detention
Sit up straight
Don't be late
Dare to talk
Hit by chalk
No fighting
More writing
Don't draw
Obey the law
Always look
At your book
Your spelling's poor
Clean the floor!
Don't move or meet the cane
That'll be a lot of pain
'Oh!' cried the children
'Here we go again!'

Elizabeth Sheppard (11)
Iwade Community Primary School, Kent

Guess Who?

Fur lover,
White cover,
Spot hater,
Dog dater,
Checkerboard,
Dog lord,
Cruella da Vil.

Charlotte Fisher (10)
Iwade Community Primary School, Kent

Autumn

Crisp leaves falling,
Crunching under your feet,
Rainy days and cold nights,
Open fires to keep you warm,
Acorns falling,
Squirrels picking them up and hiding them,
Animals hiding all around,
Autumn is great!

Ryan Luker (10)
Iwade Community Primary School, Kent

The Young Boy

There was a young boy called Tony
Who was incredibly bony
His legs looked like Twiglets
He liked to play with piglets
And that was the end of Tony.

Jamie-Lee Smith (11)
Iwade Community Primary School, Kent

The Silly Old Dog

There was a silly old dog, Sabrina,
Who liked to drink Ribena,
She had a big fat belly,
It was like wobbly jelly,
I hope you haven't seen her.

Lauren Edwards (11)
Iwade Community Primary School, Kent

Free Spirit

Floppy ears,
Fox fear,
Fluffy tail,
Injured wail,
Brown nose,
Sweet rose,
Little digger,
Round figure,
Woodcock effect,
Noise eject,
Angry thump,
Happy jump,
Vegetarian eater,
Clover sweeter,
Small home,
Circular dome,
Noisy sleeper,
Mixy weeper,
A rabbit!

Anna Marie Brookman (10)
Iwade Community Primary School, Kent

A Cat

Night dancer
Night prowler
Flesh eater
Silky velvet
Active child
Claws wild
Pointed ears
Dog fears
Sleep master
Curtain disaster
A cat.

Faye Easton (10)
Iwade Community Primary School, Kent

Who Am I?

Ghostly sheet,
Fourteen feet,
Red ball,
Crystal mall,
Old witch,
Evil snitch,
Sleeping beauty,
House duty,
Slimy frog,
Sticky log,
Animal lover,
Kind mother,
Humming bird,
Stampeding heard,
Witch's cloak,
Seven spoke
Who am I?
Snow White!

Rachel Harrison (10)
Iwade Community Primary School, Kent

Tiny Cat

There was a tiny cat
Who wore a silky hat
He liked to lay and purr
And he had shiny fur
He always sat on a mat.

James Hooper (11)
Iwade Community Primary School, Kent

Autumn

Bare, dark trees, blowing in the wind,
Leaves drifting to the dewy grass,
Spitting colours, like a roaring fire,
Orange, yellow, gold and brown.

Creatures scampering, collecting food,
The odd bird softly chirping,
Crunching leaves under my feet,
The dew resting on the grass.

Raindrops plummeting to the ground,
Falling from the gutter,
Puddles on the floor,
The damp floor's scent.

The frosty morning air,
The wind biting my ears,
The rain touching my skin,
Leaves whipping my face.

Autumn is fantastic!

Eben Graham (10)
Iwade Community Primary School, Kent

Away In The Night

Away in the night,
The silence and fright,
The darkness has come,
As I bite my thumb,
As I listen to the owls.

Sabrina Ormston (10)
Iwade Community Primary School, Kent

Spring

Spring is here at last
The Easter bunny is near
Daffodils blooming

Chickens are hatching
Their little voices twittering
The sun is shining

Tulips are red and
Bright daffodils sway gently
Bluebells are blooming

Heavy dew mornings
Sunny evenings in the day
Frosty nights, sleep tight

Mummy birds build nests
For their baby birds to sleep
Dreaming of the day

In spring the sun shines
And the morning gets lighter
Night-time gets shorter.

Courtney Ferguson (10)
Kincardine-in-Menteith Primary School, Blairdrummond

Autumn

A utumn has come - the most beautiful season
U p in the trees birds are getting ready to migrate
T he leaves are crinkly and dry with spots
U nder the ground the squirrels are stocking up
M igrating is a big task for the birds
N ights are getting longer, days are getting shorter.

James McBeath (11)
Kincardine-in-Menteith Primary School, Blairdrummond

Winter - Haikus

Falling snow is here,
Wet icicles are dripping,
Everything is white.

Bright lights are shining,
Shining like a twinkling star,
Dancing in the night.

I build a snowman,
My hands become very cold,
I put on my gloves.

Now I am warmer,
Inside beside a warm fire
My hands are now warm.

I look at the cat,
Walking gently in the snow,
She is snowy-white.

Madeleine Darby (10)
Kincardine-in-Menteith Primary School, Blairdrummond

Hallowe'en

H allowe'en is a time for trick or treating
A ll the ghosts come out
L ow in their graves the dead come alive
L anterns are magically burning out
'O www,' cries the basilisk
W e all hope we won't pass by a witch
E ven ghouls make an appearance at Hallowe'en
E very child knows that their worst fear is Dracula
N ow Hallowe'en has come!

Fraser Graham (11)
Kincardine-in-Menteith Primary School, Blairdrummond

Hallowe'en

H allowe'en is when scary ghosts haunt you for your life
A ll the vampires have fangs ready to bite
L ittle children go for trick or treat
L ots of people to go and scare
O ver the hills witches fly
W here vampires come to eat and terrify
E veryone is scared of Hallowe'en
E veryone is scared of the door at night
N ever go out yourself or you will be the supper of Hallowe'en.

Amanda Killen (9)
Kincardine-in-Menteith Primary School, Blairdrummond

Spring - Haikus

Spring is coming now,
Golden sun, heavy dews come,
Frost in the morning.

Tulips shaped like crowns,
Bright yellow daffodils bloom,
Bluebells burst open.

More sun comes to Earth,
Less dark, a lot more daylight
Light is getting bright.

Chicks hatch out their eggs,
Newborn lambs skip round the fields,
Easter bunny comes.

Birds sing through the day,
Birds sit twittering in trees,
They fly through the air.

Jaime Buchanan (10)
Kincardine-in-Menteith Primary School, Blairdrummond

Hallowe'en

Hallowe'en is when vampires come out and witches make stews.
Hallowe'en is when people make faces out of pumpkins and bats
come out of their caves.
Hallowe'en is when children dress up as vampires and ghosts and
have Hallowe'en parties.
Hallowe'en is a fun time, but Hallowe'en is a scary time as well.

Phil Aitken (8)
Kincardine-in-Menteith Primary School, Blairdrummond

Winter - Haikus

The snow is falling,
Everything is icy white,
Everything looks dead.

The snow has landed,
The children make snow people,
They come out to play.

The night is so cold,
Everyone is so happy,
Winter is great fun.

Teddi Anderson (10)
Kincardine-in-Menteith Primary School, Blairdrummond

Autumn

A utumn has come and taken the old leaves off the trees
U nder the ground, nuts are being forgotten by the squirrels
T he trees are bare and the seeds are falling
U p in the hills you can see millions of autumn trees
M igrating birds are ready to move
N ow the days are shorter and the nights are longer.

Andrew McLeod (11)
Kincardine-in-Menteith Primary School, Blairdrummond

Scary Lion

If you want to see a lion
You must go down to the long stringy grass

I know a lion who's living down there
It's a fierce one, it's a great killer
It's a fast one, it's a loud one

But if you really want to see a lion
You must go down to the long stringy grass
Go down gently to the long grass
And say, 'Lion wake up, lion wake up'
And it will chase you away
But don't stick around
Run for your life!

John Graham (7)
Kincardine-in-Menteith Primary School, Blairdrummond

Muddy Swamp

If you want to see a snake
You must go down to the muddy swamp

I know a snake
Who's living down there
It's a creepy one, it's a sly one
It's a fierce one, it's a slithery one

But if you really want to see a snake
You must go down to the muddy swamp

Go down gently to the muddy swamp
And say, 'Creepy snake, swaying snake,
Come down here'

And it will slither down
But don't stick around
Run for your life!

Louise Wilson (8)
Kincardine-in-Menteith Primary School, Blairdrummond

Vulture Tree

If you want to see a vulture
You must go down to the old oak tree

I know a vulture
Who's living down there

It's a fierce one
It's a spy tracker
It's a great killer!

But if you really want to see a vulture
You must go down to the old oak tree

Go down gently to the old oak tree
And say, 'Hello vulture
Are you hungry?'

And the vulture will say *'Aarrk!'*
And the vulture will chase you
Circling the old oak tree
But don't stick around
Run for your life.

Jack Brisbane (8)
Kincardine-in-Menteith Primary School, Blairdrummond

Family

Family means everything
Especially to those who care
Sisters dancing around having a sing
While Mum's still doing her hair
Brother's playing on his PS2
Whilst Dad's coughing, he's got the flu.

Anisa Shareef (10)
Manor Primary School, Tamworth

There Is A Troll In My Back Garden

There is a troll in my back garden
If he makes a mistake he will always say pardon
He will do a litter pick every day
If he sees a charity shop he will always give his daily pay
He has loads of jobs like walking a dog
He even looks after warthogs
His best job is an engineer
He fixes pieces that fall off the end of the pier
He has never committed a crime
He messes about with loads of slime
His mum and dad are very good mimers
He has even made a clock with a timer
That was a very good week
Then in the morning all you can hear is squeak, squeak.

Dale Jones (10)
Manor Primary School, Tamworth

The Witch's House

The old oak door of the witch's house was tiny with a golden doorbell
Inside was damp and dingy like a crooked jail cell

The cold stone floor was stained and cracked
All her rat's tails in bags and sacks

Her crooked black hat with gloomy grey patches
Was near her bedroom door with the golden latches

A canopy hung on the neatly-laid bed
On her mantelpiece was a warty ogre's head

Potions lined up on cupboards and shelves
All you can hear are the cats' screeching howls

If you go in, you never come out
Not even if you squeal or shout.

Emily Church (11)
Manor Primary School, Tamworth

School Gossip Poem

A is for Ant who wears no pants
B is for Ben who has a pet hen
C is for Cat who wears the hat
D is for Daniel who got every 2004 medal,
E is for Ellie who's got a fat belly
F is for Fred who acts like he is dead
G is for Graham who gets into mayhem
H is for Harry whose best mate's called Bob
J is for Jack who wears a rucksack
K is for Kate who hasn't got a mate
L is for Lenny who hasn't a penny
M is for Mike who goes on a hike
N is for Nat whose favourite animal's a bat
O is for Ollie who plays with a dolly
P is for Paul who has a swimming pool
Q is for Queenie who's really tiny
R is for Rob who can't shut his gob
S is for Ste' whose girlfriend's called Dee
T is for Tom who wears a pompom
U is for Una who loves tuna
V is for Violet who loves a pilot
W is for Will whose family watch The Bill
X is for Xina who works as a cleaner
Y is for Yazmin whose best friend's called Jasmine
Z is for Zack who goes quack, quack.

Jack Nelson (9)
Manor Primary School, Tamworth

Goldilocks

Once upon a time in a nursery rhyme
There were three bears
A mama and a papa and a wee bear
Goldilocks came, she was hungry for food
If she didn't get some, she would be in a mood
She saw three bowls of porridge
And she tried the first one but it was much too hot
And it burned her tongue
She tried the second one but it was way too cold
So she pushed it away as you would fool's gold
She tried the last one and cried out with glee
'Oh this is perfect, it's just right for me'
After eating all of it she felt slightly drowsy
So lay on the big bed but it felt hard and lousy
She tried the second one and it felt OK
But it didn't exactly make her shout, 'Oh hooray!'
She tried the last one and cried out with glee
'Oh this is perfect, it's just right for me'
She laid back and fell asleep
But was woken up by an ear-piercing weep
'Mummy, my porridge is all eaten'
Goldilocks ran but she was beaten
Papa bear caught up with her and said
'Why did you eat my son's porridge?
Haven't you been fed?'
'Help me! You're hurting me' she gasped
She broke away and ran away, fast.

Catherine White (11)
Manor Primary School, Tamworth

My Family

All of a sudden a dirty great
Pudding came flying through the air
It missed me ma and missed me pa
And knocked me off me chair
Me brother went crazy and being so lazy
And just lay there on the floor
My cousin Hattie who's a little bit scatty
Just ran behind the door
As you can see
My family and me
Are as cranky as can be.

Jessica Tudor (9)
Manor Primary School, Tamworth

My Pony

My pony is Laddy
He is great
I love to ride him
And just can't wait
I love to canter round and round
And when I dump him
He doesn't make a sound
Lucy and I play together
Jumping and racing games
In all sorts of weather
When we've finished
We bring them in
And go off to *sleep.*

Megan Webb (9)
Manor Primary School, Tamworth

James Bond 007

J ames Bond tries to meet his friends
A nd tries to kill people and sometimes he gets hurt.
M agnums, machine guns, rocket launchers, pistols and
E ven hand grenades
S ometimes flash grenades too.

B ond has got black stuff on.
O ddjob is a very bad villain and destroys all he sees.
N ever doubt that he will win.
D oubt him and you will die.

Connor Smith (9)
Manor Primary School, Tamworth

What The Teacher Says

School
You always have to follow the rules
Like . . .
Be good
Do as you should
Eat your lunch
And I said don't punch
Don't shout out
And stop messing about
Don't throw that rubber
I have not got Flubber
You're all dismissed
But you're staying in
That's what teachers say.

Sam Storey (11)
Manor Primary School, Tamworth

Once Upon A Rhyme

Once upon a rhyme
No one knows quite when
Catfish would write poems
This is one of them

Getting chased around all day
By the naughty dogfish
He's going to catch me
And put me in his dog dish

Once upon a rhyme
No one knows quite when
Octopus would do bad tricks
This is one of them

Making little fish so scared
I'll squash them in my tentacles
I'll eat them whole then
Eat another identical

Once upon a rhyme
No one knows quite when
Toads would write stories
But I've not time for them!

Lisa Poxon (11)
Manor Primary School, Tamworth

Snakes

S nakes are small, long, short or tall
N asty, noisy, naughty
A snake is shy
K ind when they want to be
E vil eyes has a sly snake
S ome bite you in one!

Amy Morris (11)
Manor Primary School, Tamworth

Tom The Tricker

Tom the tricker tricked the tamer,
Tom the tricker tricked the tiger,
Tom the tricker tricked the tricker,
Tom the tricker tricked the tailor,
Tom the tricker tricked the teacher.

The tamer tried to trick the tricker Tom,
The tiger tried to trick the tricker Tom,
The tricker tried to trick the tricker Tom,
The tailor tried to trick the ticker Tom too
And the teacher tried to trick the tricker Tom.

They all tried
And Tom the tricker died.

James Bennett (9)
Manor Primary School, Tamworth

Hunting

Tiger hunting in the night,
Moving stealthily towards her prey,
Blending into the background,
Deer weary,
Getting nervous,
Starting to run,
Chase begun,
Closing in,
Hearts pounding,
Pounce perfect,
Food.

Sarah Starkey (9)
Manor Primary School, Tamworth

Football

Football is the best because you get to run,
Football is good because it's the best game ever,
Football makes you fit,
Footballers wear a kit,
Football, you need to learn the skills,
Say you want to play football, you have to learn fast,
Football pitch is where you play,
Football pitch is where you learn,
Football is the best ever,
Football is so good,
Football pitch is so big,
Football pitch is green,
Football is so cool,
Football is so amazing.

Ganesh S Parmar (10)
Manor Primary School, Tamworth

Christmas

C hristmas is coming
H appiness is in the air
R oast chicken wafting round the house
I n the living room stacks of pressies
S tuff in the sacks
T ime to unwrap
M ince pies, nice and warm
A ll the kids shout with glee
S anta's been.

Sophie Dixon (11)
Manor Primary School, Tamworth

The Witch's Kitchen

Cobwebs lined with glistening rain droplets
The smell of garlic and onions in the bubbling stew
Dead rats dangling down from the bloodstained wallpaper
The worn-out wooden spoon sizzling and fizzling
In the rusty black cauldron
The witch's silky black cat
Camouflaged on the black patterned rug
By the red-hot burning fire
On the mantelpiece beautiful statues of famous witches and wizards
A bookshelf with potion books and spells, torn and dusty
The eyeballs of dead toads stand in a decorated witch's bowl
Ready for a lethal stew.

Natalie Ayres (9)
Manor Primary School, Tamworth

James Bond 007

James Bond
is a spy
and doesn't die.

James Bond is so cool
he uses guns
and has a pool.

James Bond
has a cool car
and every now and then
he might pop to the bar.

James Bond
loves lots of girls
and they have lots of pearls.

Aiden Clarke (10)
Manor Primary School, Tamworth

My Cat, Monty

My kitten, Monty is a British shorthair,
He loves to jump from stair to stair,
Early one morning around about four,
Mum and Dad come in and he ran out the door.

Mum called him and called him,
There was a really sharp frost,
She was starting to worry in case he got lost,
With him being small and black as can be,
He was so very quiet and hard to see.

Daybreak came and he still wasn't home,
What started as a sniff had turned into a roam,
She shouted, shook biscuits and looked all around,
But dinner time came and he still couldn't be found.

Across fields and lanes with tears in her eyes,
Mum shouted and shouted and gave a few sighs,
Darkness then fell and it started to rain,
We didn't think we'd ever see Monty again.

At 11 o'clock we all went to bed,
We'd cried so much our eyes were red,
Very soon after, the telephone rang,
Someone up the road had heard a clang.

Mum quickly got dressed and took another look around,
It was so very quiet - you could hear every sound,
She shook his biscuits and shouted his name,
Alleluia - he finally came.

He was so very tired and glad to be home,
I think he learnt his lesson - he was too young to roam,
Since that weekend he hasn't been out,
He's here to stay - without a doubt.

Becky Milner (11)
Manor Primary School, Tamworth

Summer

S ummer is a time when flowers grow.
U nder the stems of the flowers when winter begins,
   the roots rot away.
M arigolds' bright yellow leaves shining in the summer sun.
M onkeys swing from tree to tree in the hot weather.
E lephants squirting water feeling very hot.
R oses' bright red petals just like the top colour of the rainbow.

Courtney Frear (9)
Messingham Primary School, Scunthorpe

The Visible Beast

The beast that is visible
Is stalking through the park
His breath is very rotten
And his teeth are very sharp
His hair is very spiky
It looks like he uses gel
Even though we can see him
He can see us very well

The beast that is visible
His skin is green
He smells awful.

Keiran Lindley (9)
Messingham Primary School, Scunthorpe

So Silent

It was so silent I heard stars talking to the moon
It was so silent I heard the moon talking to the sun
It was so silent I heard my rabbit's nose twitching
It was so silent I heard my toys talking.

Matthew Taylor (7)
Messingham Primary School, Scunthorpe

Before The Swim

Blowing waves,
Calm me,
So I may be brave,
Cheer me,
Loud cheers,
Hear me,
Trying to win the race,
Give me good luck,
Make me go whooshing through the water,
Take care of me,
Don't let me die,
So I may not kill me,
Escape from the other people,
Lead me to the end,
Let me be free for my race,
I'm going to win the race for everyone,
Lead me to my race.

Joshua Chamberlain
Messingham Primary School, Scunthorpe

Open Top

An open top
A people carrier

A red Rover
An advertiser

An environment polluter
A people killer

Single decker
Double decker

A catalogue to make me
A bus.

Oscar Smith (11)
Messingham Primary School, Scunthorpe

So Silent

It was so silent I could hear the gloves heating
It was so silent I could hear the fingernails talking
It was so silent I could hear the rabbit's nose twitching
It was so silent I could hear the bed mites eating my skin
It was so silent . . .

Luke Fisher (9)
Messingham Primary School, Scunthorpe

Untitled

There once was a cheeky girl,
Who stole more than one pearl,
She didn't regret it,
But had to forget it,
That cheeky little girl.

There once was an old lady called Mary,
Who wished to be a fairy,
She span around
And fell to the ground,
That was the end of Mary.

There once was a lady called Winny,
Who was extremely skinny,
She slipped on the floor
And fell down a straw,
That skinny old lady called Winny.

Jade Harniess (11)
Messingham Primary School, Scunthorpe

Untitled

I stood in a room full of commas
And I began to pause

I stood in a room full of butterflies
And I fluttered around

I stood in a room full of anxiety
And my tummy filled with butterflies

I stood in a room full of flowers
And I started to grow

I stood in a room full of worry
And my head filled with disaster

I stood in a room full of happiness
But I still felt sad

I stood in a room full of love
And I started to blush

I stood in a room full of families
But I didn't know which was mine.

Perdita-Jayne Lancaster (10)
Messingham Primary School, Scunthorpe

Disco

Banging beats
Spinning people
Lively lights
Dancing dudes
Drunk divas
A catalogue to make me
A disco.

Chris Welsh (10)
Messingham Primary School, Scunthorpe

My Limericks!

The Fat Cop!
There was a fat cop called Bob,
Who chased the kids on the rob,
He ran very fast,
But always came last
And now he's out of a job!

Pete's Car!
There was a teacher called Pete,
Who had extremely big feet,
He couldn't drive far,
In his Jaguar car,
Cos he was in the back seat!

Deaf Ears!
There was a lady called Nicky,
Who in music was very picky,
She asked them to sing,
But couldn't hear a thing,
Because the kids were taking the mickey!

Georgia Clay (10)
Messingham Primary School, Scunthorpe

Untitled

A fire ball
A fierce flapping
A killer hunter
A volcano nest
A secret machine
As rough as a billion human beings
Claws like knives
Strength of God
A catalogue to make me a dragon.

Thomas Polkinghorne (10)
Messingham Primary School, Scunthorpe

It Was So Silent . . .

It was so silent I could hear the computer thinking
It was so silent I could hear my socks grumbling about the smell
It was so silent I could hear my rabbit's nose twitching
It was so silent I could hear my hair growing
It was so silent I could hear the book reading itself.

Shay Palmer (8)
Messingham Primary School, Scunthorpe

What Am I?

Night-time sleeper,
Morning bleater,
Hand waver,
Bell bearer,
Bedside best friend,
Driving you round the bend,
A catalogue to make an
Alarm clock!

Thomas Glencross (11)
Messingham Primary School, Scunthorpe

It Was So . . .

It was so silent I could hear a cat purr
It was so silent I could hear my rabbit eat
It was so silent I could hear the moon talking to the stars
It was so silent I could hear the trees waving.

Matthew Mettam (9)
Messingham Primary School, Scunthorpe

Untitled

It was so silent that I could hear my cat singing
It was so silent that I could hear my nose growing
It was so silent that I could hear my shoes rattling
It was so silent that I could hear my knee cracking
It was so silent that I could hear my cat talking
It was silent I could hear the stars twinkling.

Jake Crossland (9)
Messingham Primary School, Scunthorpe

The Smell Of Silence

It was so silent that I could hear a pin drop.
It was so silent that I could hear a book whisper.
It was so silent that I could hear someone scratching bark off
                                    a tree from miles away.
It was so silent that I could hear an angel sing.
It was so silent that I could hear the moon talk to the sun.
It was so silent that I could hear my socks complaining about the smell.

Andy Slater (8)
Messingham Primary School, Scunthorpe

Jake's Poem

It was so quiet I heard my socks complaining about the smell
It was so quiet I heard the bubbles talking to the dirty dishes
It was so quiet I heard the paper complaining about the staples
It was so quiet I heard the moon arguing with the sun
It was so quiet I heard the plants growing
It was so quiet I heard the bark peeling
It was so quiet I heard the rainbow rising.

Jake Marshall (8)
Messingham Primary School, Scunthorpe

It Was So Silent

It was so silent that I heard my fish talking to herself
It was so silent that I heard my ruler counting to 30cm
It was so silent that I heard my zip opening and closing.

Rebecca Catterick (8)
Messingham Primary School, Scunthorpe

Untitled

It was so silent that I could hear the moon rising.
It was so silent that I could hear the water rising.
It was so silent that I could hear the shadows dancing.
It was so silent that I could hear my rubber shrink.

Rebecca Walters (8)
Messingham Primary School, Scunthorpe

It Was So Silent

It was so silent that I heard the world slowly turn around.
It was so silent that I heard my socks grumbling about the smell.
It was so silent that I heard this poem read itself out to me.
It was so silent that I heard my bed talk to me.

Rory Simpson (8)
Messingham Primary School, Scunthorpe

A Poem To Be Spoken Silently

It was so silent
That I could hear my bears talking to each other,
Speaking about me.
It was so silent
That I could hear my clock ticking
Faster and faster.

Bethany Drewery (8)
Messingham Primary School, Scunthorpe

A Poem To Be Spoken Silently

It was so silent that I heard the moon talk to the stars
As they shined their way through the dark sky

It was so silent that I heard my rabbit's nose twitching
As it grew darker in the misty night.

Amy Cook (8)
Messingham Primary School, Scunthorpe

Before The Swimming Race

Swooshing water,
Hear me,
Slashing waves,
Calm me,
Swaying blue water,
Focus me,
Warm water,
Help me,
Win my special race.
As the waves
Go up and down,
So I may
Relax all the fears
That flow through
My body,
So I may
Be first to get
To the other side,
As all the other children
Are way behind,
I am way in front,
Swimming manager,
Lead me to the race.

Evie White (9)
Messingham Primary School, Scunthorpe

It Was So . . .

It was so silent that I could hear a sock complaining about the smell
It was so silent that I could hear the trees talking to each other
It was so silent that I could hear the breeze of the wind
It was so silent that I could hear the rain tingling.

Macaulay Farrell (8)
Messingham Primary School, Scunthorpe

The Visible Beast

The beast that is visible
Is stalking through the park,
His breath is very rotten
And his teeth are very sharp.
His hair is very spiky,
It looks like he uses gel,
Even though we can see him,
He can see us very well.

I know he's there,
I saw his three arms,
He'll gobble you up in one go,
He's got three palms,
He's after me, I know,
He's eaten my friend, Mel,
Even though we can see him,
He can see us very well.

He'll grab you by your neck
And pull you to his hole,
He'll sit and wait,
Then he'll dig you up like a mole,
He'll eat your legs like lamb,
His head is like a bell,
Even though we can see him,
He can see us very well.

Emma Wrigley (8)
Messingham Primary School, Scunthorpe

Untitled

It was so quiet I could hear angels singing up above
It was so quiet I could hear the crow's eggs crack
It was so quiet I could hear meteors crash into planes
It was so quiet I could hear the clock ticking
It was so quiet I could hear the swimming of a fish
It was so quiet I could hear the crackling of my bones.

Max Alvy
Messingham Primary School, Scunthorpe

It Was So Silent

It was so silent that I heard my dad snoring
It was so silent that I heard my socks moaning about the smell
It was so silent . . .

Lauren Spreckley (8)
Messingham Primary School, Scunthorpe

If You Want To See A Tiger

If you want to see a tiger
You must go down to the deep dark forest by the bear cave,
I know a tiger who's living down there,
He's selfish, he's fierce,
He's scary, he's cross.
Yes, if you really want to see a tiger,
You must go down to the deep dark forest by the bear cave,
Go down very quietly and say
'Tiger, tiger, wherever you are
Come to me but don't bite my arm'
And if he does, don't just stand there,
Run for your life!

Maddison Withers (8)
Messingham Primary School, Scunthorpe

Silent

It was so silent that I could hear the curtains groan
about being stretched.
It was so silent that I could hear my mum's pin cushion scream
when a pin was poked into it.
It was so silent that I could hear Velcro scream and shout when
it was pulled apart.
It was so silent that I could hear my hairclips whispering to each other.
It was so silent that I could hear my crayons say, 'Let me colour,
let me colour!'

Lauren Jarvill (8)
Messingham Primary School, Scunthorpe

Down In The Park

Down in the park
I met a girl called Louise
But she said she couldn't stay
Because she was doing the trapeze

Down in the park
I met a girl called Lynsey
She said, 'Go away
I am very wingy'

Down in the park
I met a boy called Mitch
But he said, 'Go away
I'm watching Lilo and Stitch'

Down in the park
I met a boy called Niall
He said, 'Watch out
Or I'll drop this tile'

Down in the park
I met a girl called Meghan
She said, 'Watch out
I'm going to Heaven.'

Eilish Brown (8)
Messingham Primary School, Scunthorpe

Untitled

It was so silent that
I heard my clock ticking

It was so silent that
I heard the rain talking

It was so silent that
I heard the tree whistling.

Ryan Boult
Messingham Primary School, Scunthorpe

Untitled

It was so silent I could hear
the moon talking to the stars

It was so silent I could hear
a rabbit's nose twitching

It was so silent I could hear . . .

Tyler Short (9)
Messingham Primary School, Scunthorpe

A Poem To Be Spoken Silently

It was so silent that I could hear
the leaves talking to each other

It was so silent that I could hear
my fish saying they wanted more food

It was so silent that I could hear
my teddy bears talking to each other

It was so silent that I could hear
my pencil saying, 'I want to write something'

It was so silent that I could hear
my book turning over its pages.

Olivia Parkinson (8)
Messingham Primary School, Scunthorpe

The Visible Beast

The beast that is visible
Is stalking through the park
His breath is very rotten
And his teeth are very sharp
His hair is very spiky
It looks like he uses gel
Even though we can see him
He can see us very well

He's very, very sneaky
He just creeps right behind me
He's also very hungry
And he wants me for his tea
His tail is green and yellow
He rings the country bell
Even though we can see him
He can see us very well

He smells like very old cheese
He drives a fast car
He's black with yellow spots
His car will only drive so far
He wears a long black cloak
It's covered in some shells
Even though we can see him
He can see us very well.

Ebony Peat
Messingham Primary School, Scunthorpe

Untitled

It was so silent that I heard my hamster spinning on his wheel
It was so silent that I heard my cat scratching on the carpet
It was so silent that I heard my snake say *ssssss*
It was so silent that I heard the wind whistling.

Mollie Brown (8)
Messingham Primary School, Scunthorpe

A Poem To Be Spoken Silently

It was so silent that I heard my fishes whisper to each other
It was so silent that I heard my socks say, 'I wish we weren't
on these feet - they stink!'
It was so silent that I heard the moon talk to the stars
It was so silent that I heard the Earth go round
It was so silent that I heard the bed mites nibbling at my skin.

Natasha Hoggard (8)
Messingham Primary School, Scunthorpe

The Visible Beast

The beast that is visible
Is stalking through the park
His breath is very rotten
And his teeth are very sharp
His hair is very spiky
It looks like he uses gel
Even though we can see him
He can see you very well

The beast that is visible
Is coming after me
I'm really quickly heading home
Because I really need my tea
His hair is getting spikier
It's got a lot stronger gel
Even though we can see him
He can see us very well

The beast that is visible
Is very black and white
I'm going up a tree because
He's giving me a fright
He's getting even faster
I think I'm going to Hell
Although we can see him
He can see you very well.

Daniel Waring (8)
Messingham Primary School, Scunthorpe

The Visible Beast

The beast that is visible
Is stalking through the park,
His breath is very rotten
And his teeth are very sharp.
His hair is very spiky,
It looks like he uses gel,
Even though we can see him,
He can see us very well.

The beast that is visible,
Oh your heart is beating faster,
Beating louder than a drum
And he treats you like your master.
For you now he's coming closer,
When you hear the ding-dong bell,
Even though we can see him,
He can see us very well.

The beast that is visible,
Can be seen in the sun,
You hear his footsteps coming
And your legs are frozen numb.
But you cannot scream in terror,
Although you cannot tell,
Even though we can see him,
He can see us very well.

Megan Houldridge
Messingham Primary School, Scunthorpe

Untitled

It was so silent
I could hear my cat twitching.
It was so silent
I could hear the sun talking to the moon.

Aaron Armiger (8)
Messingham Primary School, Scunthorpe

If You Want To See A Tiger

If you want to see a tiger
You must go down to the big dark rainforest
At the end of London
I know a tiger who's living down there
He's big, he's mad, he's orange, he's fierce
Yes, if you really want to see a tiger
You must go down to the big dark rainforest
Go down slow and calm and say
'Tiger ma man
Tiger ma man
Tiger ma man'
And up it pounces
But don't stay around just
Run for your life!

Elliot Ramsbottom
Messingham Primary School, Scunthorpe

The English Rugby Team

Crashing heads
Players bargain

Jonny kicked
Martin punched

Blood flowing

Jason scored
Crowd cheering

The whistle goes!

Thomas Stephens (11)
Messingham Primary School, Scunthorpe

What Am I?

Precious predator,
Stripy strider,
Puffing panter,
Meat muncher,
Running racer,
Powerful pouncer,

A catalogue to make me . . .
A tiger.

Sarah Bankhead (11)
Messingham Primary School, Scunthorpe

I Am . . .

A mummy lover,
A creeping crawler,
A dirty diaper,
A dummy sucker,
A tearful toddler,
A whining winny,
A mardy monkey,
A teddy tugger,
A milk muncher,
A snoozy sleeper.

A catalogue to make me
A baby!

Katie Brown (11)
Messingham Primary School, Scunthorpe

The Beast That Is Visible

The beast that is visible
He really does stink
You wouldn't want to meet him
And his eyes are bright pink
You try to run
Your heart rings like a bell
Even though we can see him
He can see us very well

He's got messy fur
And he always likes a fight
You are very scared
Because he'll eat you in one bite
Where has he hidden?
You cannot tell
Even though we can see him
He can see us very well.

Iain Coulman
Messingham Primary School, Scunthorpe

What Am I?

A bird feeder,
A crab breeder,

A wave wearer,
A coral bearer,

A turtle tickler,
A dolphin nibbler,

A mermaid stroker,
A sand soaker.

A fish's home
Is where shark's roam.

A catalogue to make
An ocean!

Amy Carlile (11)
Messingham Primary School, Scunthorpe

If You Want To See A Tiger

If you want to see a tiger
You must go to the deep dark rainforest
I know a tiger who's living down there
He's scary, he's mean, he's ferocious
He's nasty, he's naughty
Yes, if you really want to see a tiger
You must go down to the deep dark rainforests
Go down softly to the rainforest and say
'Anybody home? Anybody home?
Anybody home?'
And out he'll come from the grass
But don't stay there
Run home, fast!

Tia Jay Edenbrow (8)
Messingham Primary School, Scunthorpe

What Is A Cold Winter's Night?

A dull autumn day is mountain leaves on a high hill,
Rain turns into sleet,
The leaves crackle under your feet,
Winter is nearly here.

A cold winter's night is a melting shimmer on the sea,
See the moonlight!
It shines upon me.
It shines upon the golden shore.
Look in the window of the waterfront houses,
The ladies are sipping tea.

Mountain slopes whisper as winter breezes blow,
The seeds and the bulbs are getting ready to sprout,
While the brown leaves fall off the trees,
As Christmas comes, everyone is happy
And hopes there is snow.

Charlene Penman (10) & Ryan Forster (11)
Minard Primary School, Inveraray

What Is Fear?

Fear can be so strong
It can scare the shadows.
The night whispers so quietly
That not even the air
Can hear it.

What is anger?
When I am angry
It is like a huge dragon
Melting a forest
With its flame breath.

What is calm?
Calm is a deep ocean,
Swallowing me up,
Like a small river,
Running down the mountain.

Calm rushes,
Like a sparkling stream,
Calm makes me feel like
I'm on top of the world.

Euan MacDonald & Erin Moncur (9)
Minard Primary School, Inveraray

Ten Noisy Children

Ten noisy children,
Were all drinking lime,
One choked on her drink
And then there were nine.

Nine noisy children,
One of them called Kate,
She felt rather ill
And then there were eight.

Eight noisy children,
Were all in Heaven,
One went to a dance club
And then there were seven.

Seven noisy children,
Choosing a pick 'n' mix,
One fell and bumped her head
And then there were six.

Six noisy children,
All still alive,
One of them passed away
And then there were five.

Five noisy children,
Were in a boat with oars,
One fell out of the boat,
And then there were four.

Four noisy children,
Swimming in the sea,
One got nipped by a crab
And then there were three.

Three noisy children,
All went to the zoo,
One got into the lion's cage
And then there were two.

Two noisy children,
Had gone for a run,
One ran across the road
And then there was one.

One noisy child,
Having so much fun,
She didn't do her homework
And then there were none.

Charlene Penman (10)
Minard Primary School, Inveraray

What Is Moonlight?

The moonlight is a shimmer shadow on the lake,
A spotlight on the Earth.
It will guide you
Through the breath-taking dark,
Into the place you belong.

High up in the dark sky,
Treetops whisper
Like quiet mice.
Treetops are like giants
At night, tall and thin,
Sighing,
Like shivering breath from cold people.

In the moonlight
See your shadow behind you,
Run!

The moon is there to guide you,
Do not be afraid!
You're safe in the moonlight.

Emma Paterson (10) & Natalie Clarkson (11)
Minard Primary School, Inveraray

What Is Fear?

Fear is a frightening, shivering spirit!
It is a nail-biting, breathtaking threat!
Fear is lonely, it follows you
Wherever you go!

Don't look back!

What is courage?

Courage is climbing
On a steep, breathtaking,
Rocky mountain slope,
Courage is bravery!

What is happiness?

Happiness is sitting out
In the open,
On a warm spring night,
Listening to the sheep
Bleating happily!

Eilidh Elkin (10) & Sam Moncur (11)
Minard Primary School, Inveraray

What Is A Winter Breeze?

A winter breeze
Is a shivering shimmer
Down my spine.
It is a hand of frozen fingers,
Blowing slowly through the trees,
It might make you sneeze.

What is an autumn breeze?
In a calm, autumn breeze
Leaves float down,
Like thousands of tiny helicopters,
Landing down on the ground.
Leaves whisper,
Like a discarded bag of crisps,
Crunching.

What is a spring sun?

In a spring sun,
The scorching heat
Causes hot winds
That start to melt the snowy slopes,
Like ice in my drink.

Ross McDonald (9) & Ross Forster (8)
Minard Primary School, Inveraray

Rainbow

My world is a rainbow
Colouring my days,
I'm looking for the pot of gold
Below its shining rays.

Red is the fire,
That blazes on a cold winter's night,
Orange is the squirrel
That darts about the wood,
Yellow is the sun
That shines above us all,
Green is the grass
That spreads over the fields,
Blue is the ocean
That sways in the mild weather,
Indigo is the sky
That darkens at night,
Violet is the crocus
That blows in the wind.

My world is a rainbow,
Colouring my days,
The world is a beautiful place,
In lots of different ways.

Eilidh Elkin (10)
Minard Primary School, Inveraray

Rainbow

My world is a rainbow,
Colouring my days,
I'm looking for the pot of gold,
Below its shining rays.

Red is the robin redbreast
That sings in the day,
Orange is the sunset sky
That shimmers on the loch,
Yellow is the buttercup
That dances in the breeze,
Green is the freshly mown grass
That carpets the ground,
Blue is the river
Where salmon jump in leaps,
Indigo is the colour
Of a sky before the storm,
Violet is the flower
That shines bright in the light.

My world is a rainbow,
Colouring my days,
I think I've found the pot of gold -
God's answered all my prayers.

Emma Paterson (10)
Minard Primary School, Inveraray

Limerick

There was a lady from Spain
Who went for a walk in the rain,
She stepped in a puddle
And wanted a cuddle,
Then she bought a Great Dane.

Ryan Forster (11)
Minard Primary School, Inveraray

What Is Wind?

A breeze is a dry breath,
A wind is a rush of cold air,
A gale is a snaking whip,
A hurricane is a cheetah
And a wild ice-breathing dragon.

At night shadows ballet dance,
The wind makes tree shake
Like shivering people.
I make shadows
On my bedroom wall.

The autumn wind
Floats in the air,
Like boats pushed by the wind,
Making a mess in the garden
Like moles do,
I like watching the leaves fall.

Harry Thomas & Kirsty McCallum (8)
Minard Primary School, Inveraray

Henry VIII And His Six Wives

Hey, I need a wife to give me a son - what about you, Catherine
of Aragon?
You're my brother's wife, he's now gone. Will you give me a son?
No, only a daughter, Mary and you're looking older than me, so
I'll divorce thee.

Hey, I need a wife to give me a son- what about you, Anne Boleyn?
You're a pretty girl in court, come in. Will you give me a son?
No, only a daughter, Elizabeth, so I'll cut off your head and then
you'll be dead.

Hey, I need a wife to give me a son - what about you, Jane Seymour?
You are beautiful, can I see you some more? Will you give me a son?
Yes, a bright merry boy Edward and I would still be by your side
if you hadn't died.

Hey, I need a wife to give me a son - what about you, Anne of Cleves?
Show me a picture of her, please. Will you give me a son?
No, not a single one and as you're ugly as a sow, I'll divorce
you right now.

Hey, I need a wife to give me a son - what about you,
Catherine Howard?
You don't look much of a coward. Will you give me a son?
No, not a single one and now you're looking at other men. I'll
cut off your head then.

Hey, I need a wife to give me a son - what about you, Catherine Parr?
I'm getting old and I've come this far. Will you give me a son?
No, not a single one.

Poor old Henry, he then dies and Catherine Parr, she survives.

Sophie Grove (9)
North Mundham Primary School, Chichester

Once Upon A Rhyme

Once upon a time
In the magical land of rhyme
I walked past a long mysterious stream of slime
In the stream there was lots of grime
As well as all of the lime
Along my walk I saw a bright light
It looked so much like a boogie disco night
When people came out they said it was alright
But could have been better if not so bright
Again I was off on my travels
And as I went past a wood
I met the one and only Mrs Hood
Robin was doing something so he was out
But she was sure he'd soon be about
On my adventurous walk again
Only this time I thought I'd try the train
Some of the passengers aboard the train
Thought the slime stream a real pain
But they always go back again and again
Deciding that it's nearly night
And that I want to come back when it's light
I started to go back home alone
On my way back
I met an aristocrat
Who showed me exactly where I was at
She was wearing a pretty purple hat
I went back home safe and sound
I had enjoyed my adventure all around.

Amelia McLaughlin (11)
North Mundham Primary School, Chichester

The Knight

There once was a knight,
This knight wouldn't fight,
He was scared that he'd get killed.

The knight pretended he was ill
But everyone tried to make him fight still,
So one day he had to.

He put on his armour and shield,
He tried to do his special skill,
But this knight couldn't.

Soon the big day would come
And the knight would run and run.

Then the day came,
The knight didn't feel the same,
So he didn't go.

He hid in an old shed,
He didn't want to go to bed,
He said, 'I'm scared.'

He heard a yelp of pain,
The knight decided he'll be brave,
As quick as a flash he was out.

At the end he lived,
Lived to tell the tale,
You could even ask him yourself.

Georgie Jones (10)
North Mundham Primary School, Chichester

Once Upon A Rhyme

Once upon a time,
I visited a land of rhyme,
Where all the houses were made of pine
And all the streams were slime.
I walked into the dark, misty woods,
Where I saw my friend Little Red Riding Hood,
As I watched, her nan took out the rubbish bin,
The wolf came up and said, 'May I come in?'
As I walked on, I saw one of the three little pigs,
I helped him find some very thick twigs,
I asked him, 'Why do you need these?'
'I am going to make a house, my brother's making one of peas.'
I knew he was wrong but I still walked on.
Later on, I don't know how,
But I saw a pink and yellow cow,
The cow was jumping over the moon,
Singing a very cheerful tune,
When I saw my friend there was something about
Her face that made me scream
And I woke up to find it was all just a dream.

Lucy Tallent (10)
North Mundham Primary School, Chichester

Things In Life

Pears hanging,
Birds cheeping,
Cars rushing,
Web wiggling,
Trees rustling,
Breeze blowing,
Leaves crunching,
Helicopter flying.

Amy Keates (8)
North Mundham Primary School, Chichester

Cat Food

My cat loves the 'Felix' brand of treats,
Mostly it's good for his paws and teeth.
He jumps up on his little ginger paws
And miaows and pleads and begs for more.

He loves salmon, chicken, tuna and lamb,
Although he's not all that keen on ham.
But when it comes to the flavour, rabbit,
My mum thinks it's cruel so she won't have it.

His normal meal is crunchy and dry
And he's always alert when it's treat time.
So altogether he's in his best mood
When he's eating his cat food.

Rachel Delooze (10)
North Mundham Primary School, Chichester

I Can See

Buses roaring,
Toadstools growing,
Sun glowing,
Woodlice scurrying,
What can you see?

Leaves crunching,
Grass blowing,
Trees waving,
What can you see?

Beetles crawling,
Children sitting,
That's what I can see.

Joseph Furness (8)
North Mundham Primary School, Chichester

My Magic Box
(Based on 'Magic Box' by Kit Wright)

I will put in my ancient, magic box . . .
a massive flash of lightning sparkling in the sky,
a world of peace and harmony
and a unicorn as friendly as can be.

I will put in my ancient, magic box . . .
the biggest butterfly with the most glorious patterns in the world,
a happy childhood memory,
a baby's first breath and
the most beautiful fairy with glistening wings.

My box is fashioned from diamonds, emeralds
and rubies with sparkling, shining glitter on the lid
and best friends in the corners.
Its hinges are pieces of a unicorn's horn.

In my magic box I shall swim with multicoloured dolphins,
on the great shallow waters of the Maldives
and ride on the backs of many giant, friendly dolphins,
while the sun rises in the east.

Georgia Hockey (10)
North Mundham Primary School, Chichester

Squeaky

My hamster Squeaky is so much fun,
She plays on her hamster wheel till she's done,
She sleeps through the day and plays at night,
If you're too noisy she has a fright,
She reaches up to cuddle me,
Not just when it's time for tea,
She has little, red, beady eyes and a big fat tum,
I love my Squeaky, she is fun.

Samantha Robinson (9)
North Mundham Primary School, Chichester

My Dog, Monty

My dog, Monty is such a lovely boy,
He loves to play with his doggy toys,
He has a teddy which he takes to bed,
Although he's bitten off his nose and half his head.

My dog, Monty is such a lovely boy,
His best friend is Ben, who he sees every day.
Every morning they go out and run and play,
They go for a walk at least twice a day.

My dog, Monty is such a lovely boy,
Sometimes he is naughty and sometimes he is good.
I would like to know what he is thinking,
Sometimes I'm sure that I see him winking.

My dog, Monty is such a lovely boy,
When he is tired and sleepy he can be a bit grumpy.
Especially if his bed is lumpy and bumpy,
When he wakes up he is happy and smiley.
He then eats his food and drinks all the water.

Hannah Bowering (9)
North Mundham Primary School, Chichester

Family Stranger

You're my family stranger
I'm going to meet you today
You were there for me and I didn't know
You're my family stranger
I met you
After a while I didn't speak to you
Now you think you're alone
But I will always be there
Even if you didn't know.

Megan Gillings (9)
North Mundham Primary School, Chichester

I Wonder

I wonder how the weather changes?
I wonder why God made the world?
I wonder why we have different countries?
I wonder how God made us unique?

I wonder how the clouds stay in the sky?
I wonder why we have different names?
I wonder if all of this will change?
I wonder why we are like the way we are?

I wonder!

Jennifer McClelland (10)
North Mundham Primary School, Chichester

Our Solar System

T ransmitting TV
H alting for space traffic
E clipses on Earth

S moke all around
O cean of meteors
L abyrinths of stars
A ttempting to orbit
R oughly everywhere

S upersonic stars
Y awning, it's night
S pace around me
T remendous travel
E xtraordinary aliens
M ethods for getting home.

Jordan Satturley (9)
North Mundham Primary School, Chichester

The Seasons

Young plants begin to grow,
Tall, thin trees,
Unfurling new leaves,
Green stems start to show,
Slowly.

Beautiful flowers unfolding,
In the bright, shining sun,
Blackbirds chirping happily,
Children having fun,
Noisily.

Brown leaves drifting to the ground,
As silent as a feather,
In hedgerows blackberries are found,
People watching the changing weather,
Warily.

Rain and sleet hammering down,
Jack Frost comes calling at night,
Longer nights and shorter days,
The snow falls so cold and white,
Silently.

Ellie Hutchings (11)
North Mundham Primary School, Chichester

My Little Sister

My little sister is nearly three,
She screeches and she gurgles when it's time for tea,
She doesn't like this and she doesn't like that,
So she stomps her feet and gives it to the cat,
Mum gets mad and she gets sad
And the cat goes miaow and says *'Too bad!'*

Alex Andrews (9)
North Mundham Primary School, Chichester

Once Upon A Rhyme

Once upon a rhyme,
Cinderella ran out of time,
The clock struck twelve, she had to go,
Then in came Robin Hood with his bow.
'Has anyone seen Friar Tuck?
His girlfriend's run off, he's out of luck.'
Then in came a girl chased by three hungry bears,
'She's a thief!' they called, as she ran down the stairs.
So she had no choice but to run back to the wood.
And who should she meet but Red Riding Hood.
The wolf that was chasing her had rattling bones,
Though that could be because they filled him with stones.
But the poor old wolf stumbled over some roots,
And came face to face with a cat in boots.
He was ahead of his master so he gave him a call,
Surprising poor Humpty who fell off his wall.
They bandaged him up and he went on his way,
Hurrying to the ball as they were late this fine day.
So now that everyone's at the ball,
They can all have a good time after all.

Laura Kiely (11)
North Mundham Primary School, Chichester

Space Chocolate

I'd love to see the moon and stars,
The planets Jupiter, Saturn and Mars,
Most of all I'd love to see
The galaxy and Milky Way,
They are the names of chocolate bars,
They are the ones that make your mouth water.

I've been to see the moon and stars,
The planets Jupiter, Saturn and Mars,
The best things I saw were the galaxy and Milky Way,
They don't look anything like a chocolate bar!

Emily Simpson (10)
North Mundham Primary School, Chichester

What I Can See!

Wood burning,
Holly crackling,
Berries ripening,
Grass blowing,
Cars rushing,
Birds singing,
Wind whistling,
Bugs bursting,
Toadstools lying,
Pears falling,
Bees buzzing,
Rooks growing,
Twigs bending,
Leaves tumbling,
Planes roaring,
Spiders spinning,
Buttercups speaking,
Wasps stinging,
Nutshells cracking.

Liberty Rosewarne (8)
North Mundham Primary School, Chichester

A Stranger

This stranger has white eyes like paper.
His skin is like a rock.
His teeth are as blue as the sky.
His legs are as little as a mouse's.
His head is as ugly as an alien.
His nose is as pointy as a spike.
His arm is as sharp as a saw.

Joshua Johnston (6)
St Albert's RC Primary School, Liverpool

A Stranger

His back was gold like alloy wheels.
His face was blue like the sky.
His side was white like a piece of paper.

Dylan Rose (7)
St Albert's RC Primary School, Liverpool

Teachers

Mrs Stacey plays a guitar
I think that guitar will take her far
She plays her guitar down the woods at night
And gives the animals a terrible fright
She comes home from school in a flash
And sits by the fire and eats some mash

Mr Fleming is our learning mentor
He even helps Andy clean the floor
His favourite food is a sausage roll
And sometimes tomato soup in a bowl
And he is too rich to be on the dole!

Faith Barton (9)
St Albert's RC Primary School, Liverpool

A Stranger

His eyes were blue as the day's sky,
His teeth were yellow as witch's fangs,
His hands were crooked as an old man's,
His face was old,
He was as tall as a lamppost.

Kyra Edwards (6)
St Albert's RC Primary School, Liverpool

Dolphins

Look around at the ocean door
Dolphins appear at the sea.
Jumping down, splashing around,
Happy as they'll ever be.

Dolphins, dolphins wild and free,
Don't be afraid, it's only me.

Dolphins, dolphins go to war,
While the rest are on a tour.
Dolphins, dolphins, I'll set you free,
Only if you love me.

Dolphins, dolphins all around,
Dolphins, dolphins make a sound.
Dolphins let me swim with you,
Rainbow and bubbles too.

Dolphins, dolphins wild and free,
Don't be afraid, it's only me.

Aimee Lee (10)
St Albert's RC Primary School, Liverpool

Crazy Characters

Silly Milly was looking for Billy.
Bouncy Billy was being silly.
Dozy Dad was being bad.
Clever Ellie was eating jelly.
Moaning Myrtle is a turtle.
Friendly Fred went to bed.
Honey Sonny was like a bunny.
Cinderella was looking for a fella.
Snow White had a snowball fight.

Dimitri Manoussaridis (6)
St Albert's RC Primary School, Liverpool

Night-Time

Night-time is peaceful and velvet.
Night-time is soft and spooky.
Night-time is scary and beautiful like the stars.

Siobhan Mulligan (7)
St Albert's RC Primary School, Liverpool

Night-Time Is . . .

Night-time is time for soft, black bats
to spread their wings.
Night-time is time for scary, spooky ghouls
to haunt.
Night-time is time for stars to awake
and shine.
Night-time is fun
and creepy.
Night-time is when the moon
goes to bed.

Laura Morris (7)
St Albert's RC Primary School, Liverpool

The Tiger

Far away lives a fierce tiger
He creeps down in the green long grass in the night
When he is hungry, his eyes light up
And he gets his yummy snack
Carefully he puts it into his mouth and swallows
Then he licks his lips
To get the taste off.

Francesca Coggins (7)
St Albert's RC Primary School, Liverpool

Snow

Soft as the pillow that I lie on
Soft as a couch
Soft as a glove
Cold as a lolly ice that I lick
Cold as an ice cream
Cold as an ice cube
Round as a snowball
Round as a ball that I play with
Quiet as a leaf floating in the sky
Quiet as the grass
Quiet as someone asleep
White like a scarf flapping in the wind.

Emilia Carden (7)
St Albert's RC Primary School, Liverpool

Snow

Snowflakes are quiet,
Coming down from the sky, soft
Like a baby's skin.

Like a cat when you hold it,
Cold like an ice cube,
In the cold frosty fridge.

Sophie Richards (7)
St Albert's RC Primary School, Liverpool

The Nervous Cat

The nervous cat
Climbed aboard the flying mat
He was scared of heights
So he screamed and spat.

Ashleigh Case (10)
St Albert's RC Primary School, Liverpool

Racism

Everyone has feelings
No matter how big or small
Black or white
Short or tall
Skitting, hitting are some of the things we do
Not understanding how it hurts you
Everyone is different
Everyone unique
Everyone is loved by God
For this, there is no technique
We should all join together
Even if worlds apart
And shout out loud
In one big voice
Give racism the red card!

Andrew Hardy (10)
St Albert's RC Primary School, Liverpool

Snow

Snow is like
Cotton wool in the white sky
Cat's fur
Sheepskin
Snow is quiet like a mouse tiptoeing
Cold
Like a polar bear
Like a round ball of wool.

Ciara Crosby (7)
St Albert's RC Primary School, Liverpool

Winter Wonderland, Narnia

W hite witch
I nteresting place
N othing but white
T errible ice
E xcellent place
R unning rabbits

W onderful world
O ld witch
N othing but ice
D ancing rabbits
E xcellent world
R unning dogs
L aughing hedgehog
A mazing place
N othing but rain
D azzling place.

Paul Carter (9)
St Albert's RC Primary School, Liverpool

Snow

Snow is like a big ball of cotton wool
Soft
Like a pillow
On my bed
Like a woolly sheep
Snow is cold
Like a glass with ice
Like a cold tree
Waving on top of a branch
Snow is round
Like a girl's white hat
On her head.

Robyn Wall (7)
St Albert's RC Primary School, Liverpool

You!

You!
Don't do that.
You!
That's mean, stop it.
You!
Stop picking on them.
You!
No one will like you.
You!
Stop hurting their feelings.
You!
They haven't done any harm.
You!
You wouldn't like it if that was you.
You!
They haven't caused you any harm.
You!
You wouldn't like it if somebody was calling you names.
You!
Racism is bad.

Brogan Davies (9)
St Albert's RC Primary School, Liverpool

Snow

Snow is like a cloudy sky
A fluffy sheep and a baby's hair
Snow is cold like the wind flying past the trees
Blowing past me
Soft
Like a fluffy pillow on the bed
Quiet
Like a little miss tiptoeing
Snow is white
Like . . . snow.

Charlotte Bennett (7)
St Albert's RC Primary School, Liverpool

Snow

Snow is soft
Like a baby's hair,
Like a teddy bear
Cuddling a little girl.
Cotton wool like the clouds,
Like a silky white ribbon,
Snow is quiet,
Gently coming to the floor,
Cold,
White,
Like a little bunny rabbit.

Jessica Hassell-Richardson (7)
St Albert's RC Primary School, Liverpool

Jam

If you don't like jam
You must like flan
You spread lots and lots on
Until it gets sticky
If you drop it on the floor -
It gets icky!

Sean Mulligan (9)
St Albert's RC Primary School, Liverpool

Snow

Snow is round
Like a baby's bottom
A white pea on a dinner plate
Snow is soft
Like a white cloud
Like as flat piece of silky paper
Snow is cold like ice in the freezer.

Sheamus Brennan (7)
St Albert's RC Primary School, Liverpool

Racism

If life was just one colour
It wouldn't be the same.
It would be boring and
We wouldn't have
Colour again.

If I see a black person
And they're getting beaten up,
I stop and say,
'You wouldn't like it
If you got duffed up!'

If you call people names
It will hurt them in their head.
So stop and think what
You've just said.

How would you feel
If people were skitting you?
You know you wouldn't like it.
You wouldn't.
I know you wouldn't too.

Leighton Williams (9)
St Albert's RC Primary School, Liverpool

Snow

Snow is white like a horse galloping
across the breeze.
Snow is white like stars lying
in the sky.
Snow is like soft cotton wool
nice and fluffy.
Snow is cold
like ice lying down on the cold floor.
Snow is cold.
Snowflakes melting in the sun.

Rebecca Furlong (7)
St Albert's RC Primary School, Liverpool

Racism

Black people, white people, there's hardly anything different,
So less of this cruelty, they didn't want any trouble,
They can't even afford a block of rubble,
They live in the streets and live on sweets.

The difference means nothing, the cruelty means everything,
They don't skit you,
So don't skit them,
White and black are just odd colours,
So don't go and waste one.

What would life be like with only one colour?
I think the world is better with two colours, not one.
These are people's lives that white people are wasting.
Why do people do this?
They have a life like you.

People do this for fun
Because they think that their friends think they're cool,
But they aren't.
I think they are little brats
Who always get their own way,
They are verbal little rats.

Joseph Williams (9)
St Albert's RC Primary School, Liverpool

Popcorn

Sweet popcorn in your mouth goes
Snap, crackle and pop.
It tastes so sweet, it rots your teeth
And it is so golden, like golden stars.
When you crunch, it is like a dream come true.

Jamie Ennis (10)
St Albert's RC Primary School, Liverpool

Winter Wonderland

W hite everywhere
I nteresting things around
N ever sunny
T all trees swaying
E ach
R eaching high among the sky

W inter every day
O range leaves everywhere
N oisy kids everywhere
D ull and grey
E verywhere there is snow
R aging with excitement
L ike a saucer of ice
A lways cold
N ever smiling, because it is cold
D amaged things everywhere.

Cheyenne Farrelly-Treanor (9)
St Albert's RC Primary School, Liverpool

Racism

Racism is bad
And for some people
It can be sad.
Just because you are a different colour
It doesn't mean
You should get sad,
Because you are
Just the same.
I'm so small,
They think I am a football,
That's why they kick me around.

Thomas Davies (10)
St Albert's RC Primary School, Liverpool

It Doesn't Matter If You're Black Or White

'Ouch, my leg!'
'Get off the pitch
You're black - I don't want to play with you.'
'White aren't any different.'
'So leave me alone then.'

'People say there are more asylum seekers than you
And we feel bad because we're getting abused
Because of this.'

'I only came over here to escape war,
So don't think I came to steal your jobs.'

Jonathan Spittle (9)
St Albert's RC Primary School, Liverpool

Winter Wonderland

W indy spot
I cicles plot
N owhere to go
T he pure white snow
E verywhere's white
R ed colours aren't right

W onderful display
O nly every day
N ever alone
D on't want an ice cone
E verything's damp
R eally not a good place for camp
L etting animals run
A way from a gun
N ever pack your suitcase
D o you like this place?

Charlotte Jones (10)
St Albert's RC Primary School, Liverpool

Winter Wonderland

W inter one month a year
I cy every day
N othing but white snow everywhere
T rees moving
E very day it is snowing
R ivers not flowing

W hite snow everywhere
O range sea
N othing but white snow - but
D angerous things about
E ye-catching and interesting
R un with the danger
L et it rain every day
A lonely river by the houses
'N ice houses,' said the listener
D eep in Narnia.

Declan Barry (10)
St Albert's RC Primary School, Liverpool

Computer

If you're computer crazy
Then you must be
Very lazy
You take one look
At the screen
And your eyes become
A hazy screen
You clip your mouse on clipart
And try to draw a flower
But if you get bored
You could always turn off the power.

Lucy McFarlane (10)
St Albert's RC Primary School, Liverpool

Winter Wonderland

W ind blowing everywhere
I nteresting and weird
N othing but white snow
T rees covered in snow
E verywhere is white
R obins are snuggling in their nests

W onderful and interesting
O ur houses are the warmest places
N othing but snow for miles
D rifts all around
E veryone is dressed up warm
R obins flying around
L ovely snowflakes drifting down
A nd houses which have fires
N othing but coldness all around
D oors creaking on every house.

Ellie McCarthy (10)
St Albert's RC Primary School, Liverpool

Immigrant

My country is a mess
And I know yours is not.
My country is at war
And I know yours is not.
I like it over here
With you and all my friends.
But when I go back
All that ends.
When I go to town, everybody laughs,
People always skit me and point at my hat.
I have to wear a headdress, so get off my case,
Now stop bullying me and get out of my face.

Demi Weeder (10)
St Albert's RC Primary School, Liverpool

Winter Wonderland

W inter every day
I cicles and cold
N othing but snow everywhere
T errorising noise everywhere
E ye-catching and brilliant
R aging with excitement

W icked witches everywhere
O range leaves everywhere
N asty creatures everywhere
D angerous things about
E xciting and
R aining everywhere
L eaves everywhere
A nimals everywhere
N ice people all
D ay.

Sinead Carty (10)
St Albert's RC Primary School, Liverpool

Snow

Snow is . . .
A white horse galloping in the sky.
A white eye rolling across the clouds.
Soft like a puppy dog's fur.
My pillow on my bed.
Cold like the wind.
Quiet like a mouse tiptoeing.
Someone breathing.
A white bead rolling.

Eilish Sumner (7)
St Albert's RC Primary School, Liverpool

Snow

Soft
Like a cloud swishing in the sky.
Round
Like a big ball of cotton wool
Floating in the sky.
Like white blossom landing on the ground.
Cold.
Snow is cold
Like stones made out of ice.

Kyle Fayal (7)
St Albert's RC Primary School, Liverpool

The Stormy Sea

One day in a boat, I looked in the sea
When a storm came crashing and bashing at me

It chased the boat along the waves, roaring as it went
I heard a high whistle, I wondered what it was

A mighty smashing wave threw me to the floor
I only woke up to find myself at a harbour.

Jack Woolley (10)
St John's Primary School, Lincoln

Water Poem

In the swimming pool
Off to the slide, up and up I go
Swish and swash we slide
Jumping and splashing
Crashing and bashing
Whacking and whistling
Tricking, pop!
Out I came into the water!

Emma Hume (9)
St John's Primary School, Lincoln

Tidal Wave

You crash and splash,
You send things hurtling down the beach,
You go rolling over the shore,
Sucking in everything in your way,
Flooding forests green, now blue.

Alex Jackson
St John's Primary School, Lincoln

Rain

Out of the sky raindrops fall,
Into puddles and into pools,
They trickle down so quick, so fast,
The children watch as they go past.

Pitter-patter are the sounds they make,
Plopping, dropping into lakes,
They fall and splash all around,
Making all new different sounds.

Megan Taylor (10)
St John's Primary School, Lincoln

The Tidal Wave

The tidal wave
Crashes and bashes
About, turning
The water to foam,
It goes on
Causing devastation
In the coastal cities,
You don't know where
It's going, but you
Know where it has been.

Jack Longhurst (10)
St John's Primary School, Lincoln

Rain

The rain went
Trickling down my window
I went outside to play in the
Puddles, splish-splash
I rushed in because the rain was
Going ping-ping-ping off the cars
Pitter-patter, pitter-patter, the rain
Went as the clouds passed by

Drip-drop, I think the rain is about . . .
. . . to . . .
. . . stop . . .

Francis Coyne (10)
St John's Primary School, Lincoln

Stormy Sea

I look up and see,
The frightening waves roaring over me,
The deafening and thundering noise it makes,
They crash together, they're having a fight,
It sounds like a snake hissing around,
Crash!

I look up and see,
The snake like a wave hissing over me,
Crashing, bashing, you can hear it a mile away,
I hope it doesn't go on all day,
The towering wave comes and crashes over me,
Crash!

Terri-Anne Walker
St John's Primary School, Lincoln

Stormy Sea

The sea, roaring as you sail on it,
You can hear the rain going drip-drop, drip-drop,
You see the waves going up and down,
You can hear the wind hissing, whistling,
You can hear the sea splash against the rocks.

Jack Stubbs-Stimpson (10)
St John's Primary School, Lincoln

Stormy Sea

As the sea crashes at the rocks
The other end is at a trickle, hissing into a raging sea.

Whack, wallop, slam, the wave roars
To the bottom to rise once again.

Back at the top of course there's a slam,
Smash, smack, as the trickle enters the sea.

Whack, wallop, thump, then into a trickle,
The sea is finally at a finish, onto the beach.

Alice Delaney (10)
St John's Primary School, Lincoln

The Raging Ocean

The ocean rages throughout the land,
Crashing down on the walls.
The wind whistles around the bay,
While the ocean roars with might.

The water, upturns the boats,
As they try to escape from the water's rage,
Boom! The thunder booms overhead and
Crack! The lightning cracks as the boats are being lead.

Sam Hayes (11)
St John's Primary School, Lincoln

Calmly Flows The Stream

As the stream flows across the bumpy hills,
It leads across to the old windmills,
When it gets there, the noise you hear is calm,
Sh, sh.

You can sit and play,
It won't blow you away,
Don't look flash, it might go crazy,
Splash, splash.

Calmly flows the stream, going to and fro,
It starts to rain, oh no,
Everyone goes home, the stream's alone,
Plip-plop goes the rain.

Abbie Willows
St John's Primary School, Lincoln

Pitter-Patter

The rain goes splish-splash
Making puddles on the path
Do you hear the rain on
The window pitter-patter?

The rain drizzles down your window
Drip-drop, drip-drop
Making puddles
Swish-swosh, swish-swosh.

Emily Houghton (9)
St John's Primary School, Lincoln

Splish, Splash, Splosh

Can you hear the rain pitter-patter on the path?
Yes, I hear the rain splish-splash-splosh,
Can you hear the rain ping-pong on the metal cars?
Yes, I hear the rain drip-drop, drip-drop.

When we step in puddles the water splashes,
When we step in puddles the water crashes,
The rain goes pitter-patter, ping-pong
The rain goes splish-splash-splosh.

Jessica Beeston (9)
St John's Primary School, Lincoln

Stormy Sea

Stormy seas crash onto rocks
Rough waves splash onto sand
Stormy seas shout with the tide
Rough seas whistle to be heard
Stormy seas roar against the wind

The lightning cracks as the thunder dies down
Boom! The thunder changes the whole sound
The wind whistles into a hurricane
Which soaks up boats in its path.

Lloyd Day (9)
St John's Primary School, Lincoln

The Sea

The sea goes swish-swosh over the beach,
Washing crabs away,
Dolphins going up and down,
Seagulls trying to catch fish,
The sharks hunt for food.

Luke Brown (9)
St John's Primary School, Lincoln

The Waterfall

Dropping in the water blue,
Looking at the water too,
Round and round the stream it goes,
Trickling on the radiant stones.

Splishing and splashing in the stream,
It's like a great big dream,
Smelling the summer's fresh air
And sounding like a glass being
Smashed!

Sophie Primett (10)
St John's Primary School, Lincoln

In The Pool

The man dives in the pool, splash!
He swims so fast leaving ripples behind.
To get to the slide, swoosh!
All around he hears the sound
Splish, splash, splosh!

Craig Taylor
St John's Primary School, Lincoln

The River Course

The river hisses down the mountain,
Plip-plop, plip-plop, as the water hits the rock.

The river is getting faster and faster,
Whoosh . . . the water is roaring down the raging waterfall.

As the trickle shimmers down the stream,
All that's left is a gleam.

Harriet Fluck (10)
St John's Primary School, Lincoln

Stormy Sea

The water roars and falls down with a crash,
It hisses and makes a great splash,
The water does a great swoosh
And flies up against a rock,
It swishes and splashes,
Jumping up rocks,
It splashes and crashes and bashes,
And . . . stops.

Katie Duncan (10)
St John's Primary School, Lincoln

Stormy Sea

In a storm, waves crash on the rocks of a lighthouse
The huge waves roar to and fro
Smaller waves splash on the smaller rocks . . .
The storm stops and all you can hear is the gentle trickle of water

The storm starts again
Rain pours down splashing on the water
Lightning illuminates the roaring sea
Waves start crashing on the lighthouse rocks again.

Ryan Muza (9)
St John's Primary School, Lincoln

Rain

The rain trickled on my roof,
I rushed downstairs
To play in the puddles,
Splish-splash, swish-swoosh.
Pitter-patter went the rain,
So I came back in again.

David Pettit (10)
St John's Primary School, Lincoln

The Rain

The rain came drizzling down
Smacking on the windowledge,
Drip-drop on the path,
Splishing and splashing as children
Ran through the puddles.

Pitter-patter on the rooftops,
Gently spitting on the ground,
Dripping all around,
The rain came drizzling down.

Bethany Marshall
St John's Primary School, Lincoln

Night Mail

Past wire fences and busy roads,
Electricity crackling as she goes.
Wheels screeching as they turn,
So fast that they could burn.

Birds scatter as she rattles by,
Some want to race her, let them try.
Dogs bark as she passes,
Whizzing past the wet green grasses,
She speeds past a restroom, it's still busy,
Looking at the train makes you feel dizzy!

The city awakens, we're nearly there,
Getting nearer to Leicester Square,
We're approaching the station, the train starts to slow,
Brakes are beginning to glow.

The train has stopped now,
Everyone has got their mail!

Amar Nanda & Tessa Hoad (10)
St Teresa's Catholic Primary School, Wokingham

The Alligator

The alligator was scaly and green
But it could never be seen
The alligator woke up one day
And then he decided to say
'You can run, run, run, but you cannot hide
I'll have you for my breakfast, fried'
First he ate the plump cat
He thought it needed more fat
Then he ate the elephant with big ears
Who was the one who burst into tears
He tried to eat the puma called Grace
But then he came face to face
With the man and with a ping
The alligator was shot with a sling
He took him and skinned him by the tree
But took the meat home for tea!

Hannah Jones (9)
St Teresa's Catholic Primary School, Wokingham

Animals

Brown monkey, crown monkey,
Upside down monkey.

White dog, fight dog,
Doing what you like dog.

Snow rabbit, no rabbit,
Bouncing all around rabbit.

Timid cat, fiddle cat,
Always playing with something cat.

Shy horse, my horse,
Keep the noise down horse.

Slippery fish, hickory fish,
Never stops swimming fish.

Gabriella Iorio (10)
St Teresa's Catholic Primary School, Wokingham

Mouse

Mouse
Running round the house
Mouse
Meets a woodlouse
Mouse
Running away from the cat
And scared of the rat
Mouse
Eating food
Everything chewed
Mouse
Had a long tail
And ate the mail
Mouse!

Katherine Whatley (9)
St Teresa's Catholic Primary School, Wokingham

The Big Bad Bully

The big bad bully called Polly,
Teasing me about my dolly,
I want to cry,
Polly sighs.
I have a bad dream,
I try to have a dream about a stream,
I go back to school,
I have my lucky shawl,
She bullies me again,
She pushes me with a lot of pain,
I get a surprise when a teacher comes along
And she goes *bong*,
So that's the end of the big bad bully.

Stephanie Turner (10)
St Teresa's Catholic Primary School, Wokingham

The Mouse

There was a mouse
In my house
The other day
I went in
The living room
And there it lay
Its little tail
Was flickering
About
The cat came in
And tried to
Chase it out
It rested on the doorstep
It lay on
The mat
But that cat
Was far
Too fat
So now that mouse
Is our pet
Or else it would have gone to the vet.

Louisa Bellis (9)
St Teresa's Catholic Primary School, Wokingham

My Puppy

My puppy was tiny
My puppy was cute
Its skin was shiny and
It went through chutes

One morning I lost it
I looked everywhere
And where was it hiding?
Under the stair!

Daisy Driscoll (10)
St Teresa's Catholic Primary School, Wokingham

Cat's Gone!

The cat went missing, we went on a walk,
We picked out a mouse and took it for a talk.
It said it was terrorised by our cat,
Whilst it was living in a tunnel by the mat,
That a ginger paw would reach into the hole,
One hole that was rather like that of a mole,
The paw would fiddle and fuddle around,
Creating dust clouds on the ground,
The poor mouse was terrified, her size being small,
She would hear the mouth-watering name Humbug be called,
With a swish of ginger, a recoil of a paw,
The fat ginger monster there was of no more,
Then the doorbell let off its ring
And a miaow from the pantry with a unique kind of ring.
Dad took the door, Mum took the miaow,
It was all like the scuffle at church for a pew,
As Dad opened the door, the neighbours came through,
I peeked from behind Mum, my dream had come true,
Our fat ginger queen cat
Was sitting on Dad's tennis hat,
With three cute kittens around her tummy,
I gave a big hug that sucked the air out of Mummy,
I jumped in the air and gave it a punch,
My tummy rumbled, I hadn't had lunch!

Evelyn Denton (10)
St Teresa's Catholic Primary School, Wokingham

Bullying

Bullying, bullying, bullying,
I hate it,
I know how it feels because I've been bullied a bit,
You get hit, or even get pushed into a pit!
Some people might get into a fit!
You might get pushed into a puddle
And get into a bit of a muddle.

Joanna Shimell (9)
St Teresa's Catholic Primary School, Wokingham

Gone Fishing

The peg is empty, the rod gone
Cooker turned off, the light's on
No muddy boots by the mat
The house is empty, except for the cat

Knives and forks in the sink
The house is empty, not even a clink
No bright red car in the drive
The garden smells of cabbage and chive

And on the door is a note
What does it say? May I quote
You stand there doing nothing but wishing
That on the note it says 'Gone fishing'!

Laura Carter (9)
St Teresa's Catholic Primary School, Wokingham

Tiger

Tiger crawling behind a boulder
Tiger looks behind her shoulder
She spots a deer passing by
She runs at it and has a try
Lucky deer gets away
To maybe live another day.

Declan O'Riley (9)
St Teresa's Catholic Primary School, Wokingham

Goat

Goats eat all the time
But my goat eats at half-past nine
Goats sometimes eat from the bin
Goats always are fed from a tin.

Hannah Jacklin (9)
St Teresa's Catholic Primary School, Wokingham

I'm A Snail

I'm a slimy snail,
My shell is very pale,
I slither along the path,
As I see a little calf,
My mummy says goodnight,
As the moonlight
Comes down
To the ground.

Laura Thurston (10)
St Teresa's Catholic Primary School, Wokingham

Crocodile

Crocodile, crocodile
Snap, snap, snap
Bad crocodile, bad crocodile
Clap, clap, clap
He drank a pot of glue
Then he turned blue
And that was the end of him.

Laura Day (10)
St Teresa's Catholic Primary School, Wokingham

An Animal Chant

Grey dog, play dog,
Noisy day dog.

Brown horse, crown horse,
Upside down, turn-around horse.

Black spider, slack spider,
Crawling up your back spider.

Blue mouse, zoo mouse,
Climbing in your shoe mouse.

Annie McKay (9)
St Teresa's Catholic Primary School, Wokingham

The Bears' Dance

At night they come
At night they dance
The bears of the forest

From far away
You hear their tap shoes
Tapedy-tapedy-tap

From far away
You hear their songs
La-la-la-la-la

From far away
You hear their music
Da-dee-dardy-da

From far away
You hear their joy
Ho-ho-ho-ho-ho

From far away
You see the moon on the grass
Gleam, gleam, gleam

From far away
You hear their dance
Tapedy-tapedy-tap
La-la-la-la-la
Da-dee-dardy-da
Ho-ho-ho-ho-ho
Gleam, gleam, gleam

At night they come
At night they dance
The bears of the forest
Outside a moonlit cave.

Christopher Smith (9)
St Teresa's Catholic Primary School, Wokingham

What's Going On?

Pigs in the mud
Me having a thud
Lions roaring
My dad snoring

Monkeys swinging
My doorbell ringing
Parrots talking
Birds all squawking.

Just what is going on?

Thomas Eden (10)
St Teresa's Catholic Primary School, Wokingham

The Cheetah

Cheetah, cheetah
They like to cheat,
Cheetah, cheetah
They like to sprint
Cheetah, cheetah
They like to eat
Cheetah, cheetah
He's *argh!* . . . got me!

Michael Ricketts (9)
St Teresa's Catholic Primary School, Wokingham

Let's Have Fun!

I want to touch the blazing fire.
I want to touch the tune of a soft, lovely song.
I want to hear happiness and fun.
I want to see people have lots of joy.
I want to feel slimy slugs slithering along.
I want to taste fizzy Fanta bubbling up my nose.

Benedicta Gibbs (8)
The British International School of Stavanger, Norway

Senses

I like to feel . . .
The soft feeling of my dog
The silky feeling of my sister's pyjamas
The warmth of my blanket

I like to smell . . .
Warm brownies
The smell of treacle pudding
The smell of warm chocolate melting

I like to taste . . .
Ice cream
The taste of Mars bars
The taste of warm cookies

I like to see snow
To see my friends
To see my cousin

I like to hear . . .
The tweet of birds
To hear pop stars singing.

Katie Crosby (7)
The British International School of Stavanger, Norway

I Want . . .

I want to touch a lightning bolt
And I'd love to make pigs fly
Right high up into the sky

I want to feel the cold of a five pence piece
But I'd hate to feel slimy slugs

I want to fly across the sky
With all the birds passing by
A robin redbreast just flew
Right under my chest.

Amy Gildert (8)
The British International School of Stavanger, Norway

Senses Poem

I'd like to touch dragon's fire,
I'd like to touch monster's scales
And the silkiness of the clouds.
I'd like to touch the roughness of a dinosaur's tooth,
I'd like to touch the fire-blazing sun,
The magic of a wand.

I'd like to smell bread baking,
I'd like to smell sausages sizzling.

I'd like to taste fizzy drinks as they pop in your mouth,
I'd like to taste apples as the juice squirts out,
I'd like to hear the roughness of the wind,
I'd like to hear the kindness of my mum.

I'd like to see chocolate cake as it melted away,
I'd like to see the sunrise as the pink and orange are so bright.

David Dixon (8)
The British International School of Stavanger, Norway

I Like To Touch

I like to touch
The soft feel of wool
And hard pencils.
I'd like to jump up in the sky
And touch the stars
And go to Mars.

Stuart Gray (7)
The British International School of Stavanger, Norway

The Dragon

Late at night a shade of a dragon comes out
And out of his mouth the fire comes
Turning about all over the place.

Michael Suguchev (9)
The British International School of Stavanger, Norway

Holiday Wishes

I'd love to go on holiday
To see some different places.
I'd love to go on holiday
To meet some different faces.

I'd love to go to Africa
To ride on an elephant's back.
I'd love to go to Australia
To follow a kangaroo's track.

I'd love to go to Holland
To see the world so flat.
I'd love to go to Texas
To see a cowboy's hat.

I'd love to go to Russia
To see the Russian dance.
I'd love to go to Finland
To see the reindeer prance.

I'd love to go to Mexico
To get a big suntan.
I'd love to go to Nepal
To meet a holy man.

But when I'm at home
And I think of a place
It puts a big smile
All over my face.

Joshua Brown (9)
The British International School of Stavanger, Norway

Ragnarock

Loki the god
was a real snob.
He'll bring the end of the world
all the gods told.
But Norwegians of this time
remember Lokie's terrible crime.

His children bought it in time
gods now wolf had to bind.
The queen of the underworld bound
the snake goes round
and peace for now is found.

Guendalina De Luigi (8)
The British International School of Stavanger, Norway

The Moon

I look up to the sky at night
You're always there and always bright
I can see you among the stars
I wonder if you've been to Mars?
You come out late in June
And guess who you are?
You're the moon.

Elise Damstra (9)
The British International School of Stavanger, Norway

Snake

It must be fun to be a snake,
To creep along in the dark,
Hissing to keep people awake,
Always eating lark.

Clare Cuthbert (9)
The British International School of Stavanger, Norway

Moving To Different Countries

I'm moving to lots of countries
First it is from England to Norway
I meet lots of new friends
But I'll have to leave one day

Now I'm moving to the South Pole
Everything is white and very cold
The houses are strange they are made of ice
But I will be brave and bold

It's time to go back to England
But I will be leaving behind all my friends
I will write to them and
The postman will carry my letter round the bends.

Frances Jackson (8)
The British International School of Stavanger, Norway

Senses

I like to see
The glittering moon that shines down onto the Earth,
The sun that is golden.

I like to smell,
Sweet cake freshly made,
The sizzling sausages from the pan.

I like to taste
Salty crisps on hot summer days
And some cocoa on cold winter days.

I like to touch
A piece of soft material,
The soft smooth stones on the beach.

Christina Pedersen (8)
The British International School of Stavanger, Norway

A Face

When I went to space,
I saw a face.
I thought it was
An alien's face,
It was quite a funny face.

It had big blue eyes
And a red nose,
Its face was glittering gold.

I wanted to play,
But it ran away,
I ran after it,
But it ran and hid,
So I just went away.

Becky Morrice (7)
The British International School of Stavanger, Norway

I Want To Feel

I want to feel a thousand wings
and soar across the sky.

I want to touch the blazing sun
and zoom across the sky.

I want to feel a whale's back
and swim across the sea.

I like to hear the sweet chirp, chirp
of the birds across the sea.

Darren Maguire (7)
The British International School of Stavanger, Norway

Mum's Cooking Is Lovely

I like to hear the sound of buzzing bees flying in the air,
I like the sight of birds floating in the sky,
I like to taste a soft cold ice cream
I like to see the stars in the night sky
I like to smell Mum's cooking.

Sofie Reianes (7)
The British International School of Stavanger, Norway

What I Like To Do

I like to walk in grass with feet
That feel around for rain and sleet.
You make me feel like tatty shoes
And make me think I'll always lose.
Don't sit in there and look so glum,
Come on out and have some fun!

Calum Ferguson (7)
The British International School of Stavanger, Norway

The Zoo Disaster

Once a giraffe went for a bath,
But all of his spots came off on the door,
The zookeeper painted some more on,
But they all fell onto the floor.

The monkey swinging in his cage,
Fell down and started to cry,
The zookeeper was very grumpy,
So he only looked with one eye.

Ellen Thomas (8)
The British International School of Stavanger, Norway

Out At Sea

Mr Brown and his wife
Went to sea without a knife
They did in fact not realise
A creature of enormous size
Lurking in the water's deep
Awoken from her beauty sleep

'Oh James,' said Mrs Brown scared
'I think it's something big and haired
I thought it was just you and me
Alone out here in the middle of the sea
But that big thing is going to beat us
Maybe even try to eat us'

But Mr Brown he swam away
For he didn't want to be a monster's prey
Mr Brown was eaten alive
Before he could even count to five
Together with his wife Mary
They were eaten by something big and hairy

The moral here as you can see
Is never to underestimate the sea
For in the water you might just find
A monster of a dangerous kind
Hopefully this will make you see
The dangers of the deep blue sea.

Jacob Fortes-Goldman (10)
The British International School of Stavanger, Norway

The Magical Wizard

The magical wizard is a magical man,
    He lived with a lizard during a blizzard,
    He pulls rabbits out of hats whilst riding his bike
And trying to catch a pike named Mike.

Christopher Long (9)
The British International School of Stavanger, Norway

I Love My Little Sister

I love my little sister
Because she's cute, cuddly
Funny, playful
Happy and sad
Sometimes
Tickles me like today
I love my little sister!

Jade Joyce (8)
The British International School of Stavanger, Norway

Valentine

I cannot live without your heart
So let's start again
And this time, let's be smart!

I'll try and try not to lie
Not even break an alibi

You must come back
Because I know how to track
Please come back.

Christopher Nilsen (11)
The British International School of Stavanger, Norway

The Magical Hand

In Thailand,
There is a magical hand
That always planned to make gold out of sand,
But one dark night,
I went to bed,
Without being fed
And met someone called Ed,
Then he said he had a plastic head,
But I said, 'You look like my red uncle Ted.'

Richard Phonbun (8)
The British International School of Stavanger, Norway

A Fairy Secret . . .

You don't see much when you're alone,
Sitting alone on a smooth cold stone.
That's in a field, that's quiet and still,
Just over the hill, you can see the old mill.

But there's something strange going on at the gate,
You sneak over and watch and wait.
When you get closer, what should you see?
Fairies, fairies, don't you believe me?

Well, I do. They're there, I know they're there,
They're there, dancing in their lovely dresses
That were made with care.

One is red, the other blue, but my favourite is the yellow,
With long golden hair and skin like a marshmallow,
It seems hours I've watched there,
I don't do anything but stare.

But then a deer jumps over us and scares them away,
They jump up in shock and flutter away,
As they go, the yellow one drops a flower
From her lovely dress.

But she doesn't come back; they just flutter out of sight,
Maybe they will come back another night.

Christina Nadeau (11)
The British International School of Stavanger, Norway

Untitled

When the moon and stars are out,
Scattered all about,
You can hear the sound of a horse running by,
A horse as black as the night sky,
A horse as quick as light,
A horse as beautiful as night,
He'll never stop until the night is gone.

Santhiya Manickavasakar (11)
The British International School of Stavanger, Norway

Stranger

It's so still and quiet, not a single sound outside the door
Then in a while someone knocks upon the door

The stranger stomps and bangs the door and echoes
'Let me in, let me in'
Your heart full of fair and fright
Makes you shiver in the night

Then in a while the stranger stops
But then again begins.

Anna Surgucheva (11)
The British International School of Stavanger, Norway

What Is Blue?

Blue is ink, pond, pool, sky and water is so blue.
Blue is hair, eyes and bruise, uniform and cloth.
Blue is Neptune in the universe, the whale that swims in the
oceans and seas.
I wish the world could be *blue!*

Katherine Wang (9
The British International School of Stavanger, Norway

Football

I know a man who supports a team,
It is quite clear on them he's keen,
He follows their fortunes up and down,
The first with a smile,
The last with a frown,
He hopes they'll play well at home or away,
He watches for the results every Saturday,
He hopes they'll finish at the top of the table
And then he'll celebrate for as long as he's able.

Andrew Hunter (10)
The British International School of Stavanger, Norway

My Little Alien Friend

I have a little alien friend,
Who came from outer space.
He is a kind and friendly monster,
With an enormous purple face.

His nose is as blue as the sky above,
His mouth is as wide as the sea.
His eyes are as gold as the shining sun,
His ears are as small as a pea.

I really like my alien friend,
He gives me what I lack.
So when you go to outer space,
Make sure you bring one back.

Emily Morrice (9)
The British International School of Stavanger, Norway

My Old Tabby Cat

M y old tabby cat
Y es, my old tabby cat

O n my lap all day
L azy old tabby cat
D aydreams all day

T abby cat Billy
A stripy old cat
B illy is silly
B illy is friendly
Y es, my old tabby cat, Billy

C ats are my friends
A lways my friends
T oday I shall be tabby's friend.

Britt Lee Lövöy (10)
The British International School of Stavanger, Norway

Cool People

I like soccer
I like Van Nistelrooy
I like Beckham
'Cause they're soccer players

I like Sk8boarding
I like Tony Hawk
I like Rodney Mullan
'Cause they're sk8boarders

I like rugby
I like John Eales
I like George Gregan
'Cause they're rugby players.

Callum Francis (10)
The British International School of Stavanger, Norway

For Christmas I Want . . .

For Christmas I want . . .
An electric mouse
A deluxe house
A cat (but not too fat!)
An evil rat
A golden school
A big deluxe pool
A servant (but not a fool!
And it would be good if he looked cool!)
A comic about an evil Egyptian mummy
(And I want it to be really funny!)
But I will only get this if I'm very good
As you have already understood!

Magnus Hoie (11)
The British International School of Stavanger, Norway

I Didn't See

I didn't see the deep
blue sea in America

I didn't see the small
little white snow in
Sri Lanka

I just saw those things
in my country, Norway.

Nivetha Nantharuben (9)
The British International School of Stavanger, Norway

Senses

I like to touch my furry bear
and the smooth stones on the beach.

I like to hear the singing of the birds
and my friends calling me to play with them.

I like to taste sweet things
like honey and hot food.

I like to see a war stop.

I like to smell my mum cooking
delicious things.

Stefano Croatto (8)
The British International School of Stavanger, Norway

Dragons

In a dragon's lair
I dare not stare
With him so tall
And me so small
I won't be bad
Or he'll get mad.

Jack Sullivan (9)
The British International School of Stavanger, Norway

Poem Mix

I want to meet some aliens
Who live far, far away
I want to live in the sea
What would you say?

I'd like to taste the salt from the sea
I like to taste some honey from bees

I'd like to smell the smell of trees
And I'd like to smell the smells of seas

I'd like to see the giant mountains
and I'd like to see the small sparkling fountains.

Julia Sullivan (8)
The British International School of Stavanger, Norway

I Like . . .

I like to touch the snow, it's so soft
and slimy slugs as they slither along

I like to smell the burgers and chips

I like to hear the voices of people singing

I like to see my dad every day

I like the taste of bubbling Coke
and the taste of fish.

Maiken Smylie (7)
The British International School of Stavanger, Norway

Playing

On a sunny day
You come to me and say
Will you come to me and play
With me all day

Let's slide down the slide
And sit side by side
Then let's go and horse ride
Then we can go and hide

We can also have a race
There is plenty of space
I have a little case
And that can be our base

Many people can go by
And see us playing asking why
We may also see a very big guy
And all of them will hear a sigh.

Jon Toft (8)
The British International School of Stavanger, Norway

Star Poem

I am the star that squints in the sky,
I am the sky that squashes the cloud,
I am the cloud that presses on the earth,
I am the earth that squashes the worm,
I am the worm that squeezes the earth,
I am the earth that presses on the cloud,
I am the cloud that squashes the sky,
I am the sky that squeezes the stars,
I am the star that squints in the sky.

Lise Laerdal Bryn (7)
The British International School of Stavanger, Norway

I'd Like To Fly

I'd like to fly high in the sky,
With birds up there as planes go by,
I'd fly across oceans and over the seas,
I just can't believe it how high I would be.

I'd fly up high to outer space
And would touch Jupiter's, Saturn's and Mars' base,
I'd scare a big monkey that lives in the zoo,
I'd scare it like this, I'd say a big *boo!*

Sønke Benz (8)
The British International School of Stavanger, Norway

A Snow Landscape

The snow fell from the monkey bars
And melted snowmen lay flat on the ground
The cool breeze flowed all around the park
Bundles of snow fell down the slide and frost lay on the swings
Everything was peaceful and quiet
The climbing frame had mountains of snow covering it
Splatted snowballs dotted all around the park
All was calm and peaceful as Christmas morning dawned.

William Green (10)
Willaston CE Primary School, Willaston

Diamond Ice

The gentle ice upon a blade of grass,
The thin see-through glass on the gentle water,
The cold breeze in the brittle morning,
Pavement glittered in silver leaves sprayed on the floor,
Children's laughter and playing hours on end, slipping,
Trees droop and bare in the cold winter's night.

William Mellor (10)
Willaston CE Primary School, Willaston

Snow Outside!

I raced outside
No one was there
No sound was there
Except from a gentle tweet
I sat on a park bench . . .
And shivered . . . and waited
It started to snow
Children rushed outside
Voices everywhere
Snowballs flying
At the end of the day
No one was there
No sound was there
Except for a gentle tweet
Here and there was a snowman
And the crystal-like puddles were broken
The snow-covered trees were bare.

Hannah Bramley (9)
Willaston CE Primary School, Willaston

Wintertime

The rain falls down, the fog wraps around,
Mist covers all the ground.
Up to Heaven shines Christmas lights,
Through the darkness of the night.
Up above, the moon shines down,
Even still the rain falls down,
Wonder shimmers in the night,
See the darkness all afar.

Philip Mellor (9)
Willaston CE Primary School, Willaston

Skater Boy!

Drooling on the window
He stopped, stared and looked
A monster of a skateboard
Waiting to be took
Tugging his mum's coat
They walk into the shop
'Put it on your Christmas list'
'But Mum I want it now!'
She walks up to the till
And stares at the bill

Two months later
The board is scratched and scraped
And mended with a lot of good quality grip-tape
Grinds, stalls and flip tricks
Were accomplished in a hoard
And everyone agreed it was a very good board

Two years later
Skateboarding is boring
So *boring*, everyone is *snoring*
As for the skateboard, a once much treasured toy
It was put in the bin and forgotten by the boy
The *one*, the *only*
Skater boy!

Graham O'Sullivan (11)
Willaston CE Primary School, Willaston

Appreciation Day

As a boy I was fit and healthy,
The top boy in school at tennis,
I had thousands of trophies all glimmering,
And shining in my closet of pride.

By the time I was twenty I was bold and brave
And when I began to play professionally
I felt like shouting out with joy.

To play at Wimbledon by 35
Had me bursting with pride,
I hit the ball hundreds of times
And I held the trophy up high.

But now I'm old and frail
And no one knows my name,
It seems quite sad to look back
At your finest fame in your final hour,
Such shame.

Luke Homan (10)
Willaston CE Primary School, Willaston

Christmas Time Is Here

The whispering winds whipped
Your whispering footsteps crunched in the cold white snow
The water frozen over with a white blanket
Hills are like soft white pillows
A spider's web on the front of a house glistens
As if there were a million diamonds
Small polar bears are walking around the ice-cold sea
Unable to dive in the water
And its shadow following every movement
That the polar bear is making.

Ben Cawley (9)
Willaston CE Primary School, Willaston

A Lasting Tribute

My small, gummy hands reach for the wrapping,
What's inside? Is it something for napping?
With brown floppy ears and two shining eyes,
My new toy is so soft - what a surprise!
I pick him up and hold him tight
And say, 'I'll cuddle you tonight!'

For weeks he's a favourite, for months, for years,
From time to time, out come his ears.
We sew them back in and I hug him some more,
He's definitely wearing, that's for sure,
He'll always rule over other toys,
He's just right for me, no other girls or boys!

Bimmah's fluff is falling out, but his eyes are still as bright,
As I remember the day I got him, filled with delight!
His tongue is ripped and his tummy is bare,
Where fur used to be but now isn't there
And now he's getting old, he really needs a rest,
But I don't care,
Because Bimmah's the best!

Rose Jones (11)
Willaston CE Primary School, Willaston

Magic

Floating, flying, changing, gliding,
These are the things magic is providing,
Whether you're big or whether you're small,
Magic will help you know it all,
It has been around for hundreds of years,
Bringing laughter, bringing tears,
Many stories have been told,
Some are new, some are old,
But magic was created for
The fact that it will live for evermore.

Joe Adamou (10)
Willaston CE Primary School, Willaston

Stalked

The night is dark and the light is dim
And Jenny's being followed by him, him, him.
As Jenny walked around, fear stalked the ground.
She turned round slowly but nothing was there,
It was all so very dull and bare.

She continues to walk, but she's still being stalked
And Jenny's being followed by him, him, him,
The footsteps were gradually getting louder until it came to a jolt.
She peered around, as if there was an alligator on the ground.

As she turned back, there was a shadow of black
And Jenny's being followed by him, him, him.
As her heart grew colder, a hand touched her shoulder.
'Hi Jenny, it's Dad, come to walk you back.'

Jennifer Ebbrell (11)
Willaston CE Primary School, Willaston

Casper's Memory

I am the lonely ghost
I want to remember the most
The lovely life I had
But now I'm really sad
I loved the great green Earth
The second my mum gave birth
I was the luckiest boy
With my brand new toy
I went to play in the street
With all my friends to meet
Then the street racer came
And now I look back in shame
That's the day I died
My mum wept and cried.

Calvin Deer (10)
Willaston CE Primary School, Willaston

The Native

His face tells a tale
Of the sadness he has seen.
The scars on his face,
Markings of hate.
Deep intense, hollow eyes,
That have seen battles
Over land,
His land.

The jewellery he wears
Shows a commitment of honour,
To the gods always watching over him.
The native's hair rugged and old,
Telling tales of cold winters,
The wrinkles in his skin,
Like carvings in a great sequoia tree.

The spear he holds,
He is watching for white men,
The ones who killed his kind,
His family,
The great earrings that hang low from his ears,
Showing pride and dignity.

His mouth stays shut,
But everyone will bear his story,
His face tells a tale,
That the world will soon know . . .

Becky Smith (11)
Willaston CE Primary School, Willaston

The Rainforest

A sprawling mass of blue and green
The greenest hell a beautiful scene
Down amongst this bustling life
Live some creatures with teeth like knife

Sleek bodies of jaguars that rule the ground
Stalk below the canopy without a sound
The hunted or hunters add to the din
Piranhas in shoals hunt as they swim

Birds of all colours, shape and tone
Fly though the trees with a song of their own
Swinging from branches and sliding down trees
Hopping and climbing chattering monkeys

Caimans are hiding in wait for their prey
Scanning the water in a diabolical way
As the sun sets and it becomes night
Demons and spirits begin their unorthodox flight.

Robert Eccles (11)
Willaston CE Primary School, Willaston

In Egypt . . .

The sun was burning hot
I felt like a boiling pot,
I heard a sound on the ground,
Moan, groan, pardon me,
Look, a golden stone for you and me,
Down in the base,
Down the staircase,
Then I saw a huge wall,
It was 6 metres tall,
It was the tomb of Tutankhamen,
We broke the wall with a drill,
What we saw next was a thrill.

James Whitehouse (9)
Willaston CE Primary School, Willaston

The Car Of My Dreams

I have always simply imagined myself in this supreme beauty,
Me behind this steering wheel beats anything, it's the best,
I cannot believe I'm sitting on pure leather of a serpent,
The outside glossy coat totally merges into everything,
This is a noble beast.

As I drive this car I scuff my dream car,
I press the satellite navigation but it doesn't please,
This car doesn't grab my attention, as long ago it did,
Suddenly I miss hit a peddle and collided with its enemy,
A bruised and battered beast.

I always thought the dream of my life would hold my pleasure forever,
But that has failed to be,
Now I stand and watch this car rot away,
As the stench of leaking oil reaches my nose,
Now I walk away.

Chris Hall (10)
Willaston CE Primary School, Willaston

The Egypt Poem

The sun is beaming down on me and I cannot open my eyes
I stumble and look down to see where a carved stone lies
I go down the steps and it gets colder
I lit my candle, could it be?
A wall was right in front of me
Could it be the thing I need to see?
I fought my way though the cold, thick wall
And I saw a mummy case,
Jewels, rubies and pearls and diamonds,
I was astounded by it all.

Stephanie de Jonge (8)
Willaston CE Primary School, Willaston

Fifty To One

Fresh from Britain stood 50 young men in the back-ups,
Older soldiers with one arm or leg stared at them from the front.
The new recruits scanned their mud-splattered home,
Drinking some tea from old chipped cups.
When the first attack dawned on them they
Moved much quicker than the older ones stagger.
As the blasts came from the Germans everyone scattered
And the shot ones were carted away.

As the months passed by and the new recruits poured in,
They grew slower and some had passed away.
Their energy had reduced and so did the rations,
The lowest sounds had become an awful din.
Muddier the 8ft high trenches became
And so did the khaki the English wore.
In came the bombs, bullets and grenades,
Even more had died and who was to blame?

Within a year or two, the fifty that was,
Is now a half-dead group of one or two!
Down they had come like flies in a room,
Every day the battle was hard 'twas.
50 went down to one and he was in his bed,
As the Germans came over and rattled the English line.
They went in the tents and took prisoners back
And took the old one and shot him *dead!*

Max Eastwood (11)
Willaston CE Primary School, Willaston

Photo Album

Alone she sits in her favourite chair
Turning the pages and looking there
A tear comes into her deep blue eye
Oh Albert, why did you have to die?
Looking at her wedding day
And honeymoon at Majorca Bay
The long walks she had in the park
As the air gets cold and the night gets dark

All the holidays she's ever had
The ever so good ones, the ever so bad
Her little girl as good as gold
Only a couple of minutes old
And then her daughter's wedding day
Her favourite time in early May
Her daughter's died and so has he
Now no one's left but lonely me.

Tasha Whorton (10)
Willaston CE Primary School, Willaston

The Egyptian Discovery

There's no shade anywhere and my hair is sticking to me.
A stone with strange carvings on. What can this be?
Brushing away all the sand, excitement in the air,
As I follow the steps in darkness, a cool rush of air lifts my hair.
At the end of the passage I come to a wall,
Is this it?
I push and shove, soon the wall gives way,
Inside the tomb, golden jewels lay,
Toys and jewellery, a golden mask,
This is it, the end of my task.

Emily Straiton (9)
Willaston CE Primary School, Willaston

The Amazing Discovery

The Egyptian land is dry and hot, it's dry and hot.
The sensation of sand rubbing on me,
I looked down and saw an ancient stone, deary me
I'm going down, it's cold and dark,
Excited, I see a light appear,
Before me stood a wall, could it be an ancient tomb?

Bang, crash the wall goes, the sight behind was so amazing,
Gold so dazzling it nearly knocked me over,
I was as lucky as a four-leafed clover.
I gasped, it was a wonderful sight
And then I had an awful fright,
In my sight I saw a decayed body,
I screamed, I ran, I lost him,
Lucky me.

Jonathan Crick (9)
Willaston CE Primary School, Willaston

Mothers Chatting

Mothers always chat,
They talk about
Fights and bites and rights,
They talk about
Trains and Danes and
People selling houses by Reeds Rains,
They talk about
Cheese and knees and
The next-door neighbour's dog that has fleas,
We tell them to stop but they just do it more,
So let's give them a shout,
Give them a roar
Stop chatting or else we'll confuse you
By speaking in Latin!

George Wilkinson (9)
Willaston CE Primary School, Willaston

Tutankhamen's Tomb

The hot desert sun is dazzling and burning on my face,
I tripped over my hot black lace.
I looked down and saw a staircase,
Before my eyes I saw a wall.
I wondered *could it be the pharaoh's tomb?*
I found a stone and picked it up
And threw it at the wall,
Behind the wall were jewels, a mask and a crown.
I walked into the middle,
There was a golden box,
I blew the dust off,
It was Tutankhamen's tomb.

Robyn Whorton (8)
Willaston CE Primary School, Willaston

Flight

I look into the sky I see a shooting star,
Looking like a diamond in the sky,
It is going very far
And makes me feel like jumping out to fly,
To whizz through the clouds in the dreamy mist.
I would be a phoenix and burst into flames,
I'd be the number one bird on the list.
Swooping and flying over the river Thames,
I would glide through the air like swimming in a pool,
Then I would go back to my nest,
Feed my cheeping babies and settle to rest.

Tara Hatton (9)
Willaston CE Primary School, Willaston

The Tomb Of The Pharaoh

It's way too hot, way too hot, bright blue skies,
With scorching sun, it hurts my eyes,
But wait . . . what's this, a cuboid block?
Could it be a solid gold rock?

I'm going down, do you want to follow me?
Wait . . . it's pitch-black I can hardly see,
Oh no, a wall standing strong,
How do I get in? Will it take me long?

Aha, a tiny hole, it's so small,
Will this be the key to get through this wall?
Whur, whur, clatter, bang, crash!
The wall's coming down with a great big smash.

Wow, great, yes, yes, yes!
Tutankhamen's tomb and mummy in a bandage dress,
Gold, jewels, weapons and sledge,
Sarcophagus, toys and mask to the edge.

Bethan Currie (8)
Willaston CE Primary School, Willaston